Unlock Your Mind

Rewire Your Brain to Gain Massive
Confidence, Success, and Instant
Influence

Marczell Klein

Do More Books: Books That Inspire

CONTENTS

PROLOGUE   1

The Milgram Experiment, 1961   3

1. Mr. Wright - The Man Who Cured Cancer With His Mind   11

2. How Adolf Hitler Turned Germany Into a Killing Machine   23

3. The Civil War and the Morphine Shortage   34

4. Galina Korzhova, The Charming Thief of Moscow, Russia   44

5. Galina Korzhova, The Charming Thief of Moscow, Russia (SPLIT)   56

6. Sigmund Freud and the Oedipus Complex   58

7. Benny Hinn - Faith Healer   70

8. Marty Homlish and SAP, early 2000s   79

9. The US Military in Vietnam   89

10. James Fitzgerald and The Unabomber   97

11. King Louis and The Mesmerized Painter   106

12. Final Thoughts   118

PROLOGUE

When I had the opportunity to change my mindset and gain true confidence and control of my life, I said yes. And my life dramatically changed. I now have the ability to make more money, buy more things, and influence people, but more importantly for me, I have the ability to help other people, like you, to change their lives. I have gained ultimate authority over my own life. At the time of writing this book, I have earned tens of millions of dollars and helped thousands around the world transform their lives, their finances, and their relationships — just by learning how to gain true confidence.

The crazy part is that it's not like I am teaching people to be like me. I've devoted my life to becoming the best hypnotist in the world, but most of the people I have helped are business owners, entrepreneurs, CEOs, and other professionals that have benefited from learning how to gain true confidence and a limitless mindset.

It all starts with teaching them how to harness the incredible power that they already have inside of them — their mind. I want the same thing for you. The whole reason I wrote this book was to provide a blueprint for anyone who wanted to take control of their life.

If you're ready to do that, let's go.

THE MILGRAM EXPERIMENT, 1961

M ost of us are extremely unaware of the evil things we are capable of doing. We like to think that the world is a good place and that of course we ourselves are mostly good. The problem is that's a lie. More people are capable of evil than you would like to believe.

Let me ask you a question.

How many people do you think would commit murder simply because they were told to do it? Would it be a small or large percentage of the population? Take a look at the people you know, maybe someone you pass on the street — do you think someone you know would kill another person for no reason? Probably not.

Well, in the year 1961, Stanley Milgram asked himself a similar question. How could an entire country, such as Germany, stand by when a holocaust was occurring?

Did the citizens not know what was going on?

When officers or the SS from the Nazi regime were questioned about their war crimes, they were asked why they did such horrible things, and the response was nearly always the same: "I was just following orders."

This response baffled Stanley Milgram. He was amazed that a human would obey orders even if they conflicted with their personal values — *simply because an authority figure told them to do it.* In order to test this theory, he decided to conduct an experiment based on one simple question.

Would a human kill another human simply because an authority told them to do it?

The idea was simple. He would introduce himself as a doctor to a test subject and tell them the following idea. *We believe that electric shock therapy will improve someone's ability to learn.* The subject would then be assigned the role as a teacher and be given a simple task — to ask someone questions and if the answers were wrong, then they had to shock them. The more wrong answers, the higher the lethality of the shock.

There was one catch. If you were uncomfortable with potentially administering a deadly shock to the student, you could leave — but you would fail the test. With the instructions given, the teacher would settle into their role. As they asked the first few questions, everything seemed to go smoothly. No wrong answers meant no shocking. But then the student would start to get questions wrong. 5 volts... 10 volts... 50 volts.

By the time the student had missed five or six questions, the teacher was visibly uncomfortable administering the electric shock. 100, 125, 150 volts. By the time the student was at ten or more missed questions, it was impossible to ignore the student's screams from the other room.

"Please, my head hurts!"

"I have a family!"

Despite the obvious suffering of the student, 68% of all the people continued to the maximum and entirely deadly voltage of 450 volts. They were willing to commit murder because someone in a lab coat told them to do it. Milgram's experiment has been performed and documented at least forty times since he first introduced it, and the results are always the same. It didn't matter their religion, their beliefs, or their education level; over 68% of the people tested were willing to potentially kill someone because they were told to by someone in authority — even if they didn't agree.

This study needs to be reviewed by every single person in the world because of the major implications it has to your life. Of course, you are telling yourself that you are part of the thirty percent that would never do such a thing. That's what everyone says — and should say — but statistically, you would.

Even if you were part of the thirty percent that refused to administer the lethal 450 volts, that means you were a part of the thirty percent that stopped at 250 volts which was still more than enough to kill someone.

In other words, *one hundred percent of the people in Milgram's experiment were willing to kill someone* — simply because they were told to by someone they perceived to be in authority. To make it more personal, one hundred percent of the world, including you and me, are willing to kill someone simply because we were told to do it.

Perceived Authority

The biggest problem is that Milgram's experiment did not provide any solutions. That's because his study only focused on one percent of the problem — the actions that the people took. The next step he should've taken is asking *why.* Why were the people willing to kill? Why did they obey? Why did the others refuse to kill? The answer is this: humans have a deeply rooted instinct to respond to authority. This instinct goes back millions of years to our tribal roots.

Disobeying your leader back then meant beheading, execution, or expulsion from the tribe — which meant almost certain death. Your subconscious mind thinks that you will die if you do not follow instructions. That's why most people will blindly follow whatever authorities tell them to do because your subconscious mind is more willing to kill a stranger than sacrifice your own life. In other words, you might be living a life completely based on what your government, religious leaders, society, and your family tell you — *even if you know it's wrong*.

What Milgram's Experiment Showed Us

Ultimately, what Milgram's experiment revealed is that humans are capable of great evil. No matter what their values or beliefs are, the majority of humans would rather obey authority than stand up for what they believe. Values and beliefs will almost always go out the window when your life is on the line.

This is possible because people in power have found out that they can control other people's minds better than they can. How do they do this? It's all about creating perceived authority. Perceived authority is the ability of someone to create a sense of authority in our life. America, despite its protests, has a perceived authority of cops. If they give directions, the majority of people will comply. However, if you go to other countries, people will literally spit on cops and completely disregard anything that they say. In those countries, being a cop carries no perception of authority. This is also the idea behind religion.

Most religions have the belief that God is the ultimate authority. Because of this perception, religious leaders can also gain authority because no one wants to argue with who God "puts in authority." That's why cult leaders can convince their followers to drink poison, governments can make soldiers kill without asking why, and a leader like Hitler can convince an entire nation to kill their neighbors — all because of perceived authority.

Authority Is Necessary For Control

Now, not all authorities want you to kill innocent people, but they do want to influence your life. Your religious leader wants you to act a certain way, your parents want you to get a certain job, and companies spend a lot of money on ads convincing you that you need to buy a certain product. And while their goals may be different, they all use the same tool to control your life. Authority.

Now, if you're okay with that — with people controlling your life — then stop reading now. This book isn't for you. But if you want more out of life, if you want to learn how to influence people and walk into any situation with the authority and ability to get what you want, then you should keep reading.

Imagine a tool so powerful that it literally gives you the power to do anything that you can dream or imagine. Now imagine that someone hijacked this tool and started using it for their own good. That's where most of us are living today. Our minds have been hijacked and our power has been stolen from us. Instead of making ourselves money, we make others money.

Instead of living our dreams, we try to follow others. That's why we need to take back our minds and start using them for the things we want to do. But before you do that, you have to break out of the trance (or matrix) that you've been stuck in for so long.

Using Authority For You

The idea that people are abusing authority every day and are even using it against you right now is pretty unsettling, but it also presents you with a unique opportunity. First, you should be angry that people are doing this to you, but then you should ask yourself an important question. *What if I were able to have this kind of authority?* What if you were able to use the same tactics and tools that governments use to subconsciously brainwash their citizens — but instead of using it for bad, you used it for good?

How would your life change?

Imagine walking into a room and immediately being able to take charge. Imagine how much more money you would be able to make if you were able to consistently use the person's innate desire to follow others to your advantage. Would you be more successful? Would you have more impact?

Before you continue, I need to make a disclaimer: I am not responsible for what you use this incredible power to do. These concepts are so powerful that, when mastered, you will be able to convince almost anyone to do anything — *even if it goes against their will.*

My hope is that when you master these concepts and techniques you will use them to accomplish your greatest dreams and make the world a better place.

1

MR. WRIGHT – THE MAN WHO CURED CANCER WITH HIS MIND

The Power of Your Mind

In 1957, there was a man who had an advanced form of cancer called lymphosarcoma. All treatments had failed, and time was running out. The man's whole upper body was filled with tumors from his neck to his groin, his internal organs were enlarged, and the cancer cause his chest to fill up with nearly two quarts of milky fluid everyday – which had to be constantly drained just so he could breathe. His doctor, Dr. West, did not expect him to live longer than a week.

Despite his awful condition, the man — called Mr. Wright — desperately wanted to live and insisted on his doctor treating him with a new clinical drug called Krebiozen. The drug was only offered as a clinical trial to those that doctors believed had at least three months left to live, but Mr. Wright wouldn't give up. Knowing that this drug would be his miracle cure, he kept begging his doctor to give him a dose of the drug.

Finally, the doctor agreed and was able to inject him with Krebiozen. Surprisingly, the following Monday, just three days after being injected with the clinical drug, Mr. Wright was able to get out of bed and walk. According to Dr. West, "the tumor masses had melted like snowballs on a hot stove" and were half the original size. Ten days after the first dose of Krebiozen, Mr. Wright left the hospital free of cancer. The next two months, he enjoyed life and couldn't stop talking about the miracle drug, Krebiozen.

Mr. Wright was healed.

Then, one day, he started to read scientific literature that suggested that Krebiozen didn't seem to be effective. Mr. Wright believed the reports, became extremely depressed and his cancer came back.

When he returned back to his doctor, Dr. West attempted to restore his patient's faith in the drug. He told him that some of the initial shipments of the drug had lost their strength, but he had a new batch of highly concentrated, pure Krebiozen. (It was a bold-faced lie, but Dr. West hoped it would give his patient hope.)

Following the lie, Dr. West injected Mr. Wright with the "new Krebiozen," which was nothing more than distilled water. Incredibly, the medicine had the same result. The tumors left, the fluid disappeared and he returned home.

Mr. Wright was healed again.

Then the worst thing possible happened — The American Medical Association announced that a nationwide study of Krebiozen proved that the drug was completely worthless. (It ended up that the creator of the drug, a Yugoslavian physican called Stevan Durocic, was a fraud and the medication was nothing more than mineral oil and creatine.) This time, Mr. Wright lost all faith in his treatment and Dr. West couldn't restore his faith in the drug. The cancer came back, and he died just two days later.

Understanding Your Subconscious Mind

In order to fully understand this story, you have to understand how the mind works. I already gave you the first step — learn to focus on the subconscious mind.

Now, that sounds simple, but again, the problem is most people never learn to distinguish between the conscious and subconscious — much fewer learn to access and rewire their subconscious mind.

Your conscious mind is capable of processing about 150 bits of information per second. As good as that sounds, your subconscious mind is capable of processing 50 million bits of information per second. Just imagine that, until you learn to tap into your subconscious mind, you are only using less than a hundredth thousandth of a percent of your mind or .00001%.

That's pretty insane! But that's exactly what most of us do because we don't understand how our mind works. The mind is essentially a computer.

Based on the programs you run, the apps you download and yes, even the viruses that are present, your mind either runs efficiently and with your best interests in mind or it runs slowly and is actually self-sabotaging with every program it opens. In the case of Mr. Wright, he was programmed to believe the medical experts and everything they said — that program would end up killing him.

Beta vs. Theta

Your mind has different brainwave states from when you are asleep to when you are entirely conscious. For the sake of this lesson, we will focus on just two: beta and theta. Let's start with the latter.

Theta is the brain wave state that is most common in children under ten years old. When you are in theta, your mind is highly receptive to new information, making it easier to learn new languages, adopt new behaviors, and absorb new ideas.

However, as you get older, your brain shifts into beta. Beta is a state that is less conducive to learning and more focused on executing established patterns of thought and behavior.

The problem with operating in beta is that the patterns of thought and behavior that were established as a child are deeply ingrained in your brain so your entire mind is operating on the mind of an 8-year-old.

In the case of Mr. Wright, he was so heavily programmed to believe that the medical experts were always right — even if it went against his own experience. This inability to accept the facts versus his belief in science and the "experts" canceled out the reality that he was healed from cancer. That's how influential the thoughts and patterns that are established in our theta mode are.

Breaking the Patterns

There are only two options when you are looking to break the patterns and beliefs that were ingrained in your mind. The first approach is forming new habits through intense focus and repetition. This approach can work, but the amount of time and effort it takes to create new neural pathways in your mind is extreme. By the time you have broken your old habits and instilled new ones, you will have lost valuable time and money.

The damage created in your life will be much more difficult to overcome. The shortcut is to re-engage the theta state of your mind. When you have figured out how to do this, you are able to drastically shorten the amount of time it takes to form new patterns in your mind.

Your Critical Faculty

In order to sort through the massive amounts of data that your mind processes every minute, your brain installs a filter between your conscious and subconscious mind. This filter is called your critical faculty. While your mind is in a theta state, it hasn't developed the ability to think critically. It's like a sponge soaking up everything you see, hear, and experience.

Your views on money, the world, and love will solely be influenced by your experiences up until the age of ten. After this, your critical faculty begins to filter this information through the things you have experienced. This can be a good thing and a bad thing.

Imagine watching a movie where someone commits a murder. Now, if you saw a murder in real life, you would have some kind of reaction based on your beliefs and values. Most of us think murder is wrong, so if we saw a murder in real life, we would feel inclined to do something. Maybe we would run away, call the police, or intervene to try to stop the murder from happening. However, if the murder takes place in a movie, you won't do much of anything.

That's because your mind has critically analyzed the data. It knows the movie is not true and that you can enjoy the rest of the movie without worrying about the murder you just saw. Because it's in a movie, you might even start discussing whether or not you would have killed someone if you were that character.

This happens in your mind every time it receives data. If you are given an opportunity to make money, your mind filters it based on everything it's already experienced and learned in life. If you meet someone who could potentially be your life partner, it will filter it based on your previous experiences and memories of past relationships. Depending on your experiences, this filter could lead you to success or failure.

Deleting Bad Programs

The key to fine-tuning your critical faculty is to delete bad programs from your mind. Imagine being able to travel back with a time machine and delete the painful memories and experiences that have held you back for so long. Where would you go? What would you change? I want you to close your eyes and imagine the place, the time, your age, and the memory. Now just hit delete on the memory and replace it with a good one — one that serves you better. Sounds crazy right?

This is possible!

Our mind is constantly deleting data every day. It also deletes amazing opportunities to fulfill your wildest dreams because it doesn't fit with your ten-year-old programming. In order to unlock the superpower of deleting memories and opening your mind to see the opportunities around you, your mind must re-enter the theta state. Another word for theta would be a trance.

A trance is simply a state of being where we are hyper-focused on one thing. A trance is a place where we are also more susceptible to suggestions. For Mr. Wright, he was hyper-focused on the drug Krebiozen healing him from cancer. He was so focused on it that he was actually healed... Twice! Again, this is a good thing and a bad thing.

While in a trance, the things that are suggested to you are extremely powerful. If you are in a trance and someone suggests something dark and evil, you are more likely to do it. But the opposite is true as well. If you are in a trance and someone makes a positive suggestion, again, you are more likely to do it.

The first step in reprogramming your mind is learning to bypass your filter and start opening your mind to the possibilities and opportunities that have been all around you. But again, I need to stress the importance of being highly cautious of who and what you allow to enter your mind while you are in this highly suggestible state.

When you're in a trance, your mind deletes things. It deletes memories and opportunities. Deleting memories can be a good thing. Deleting opportunities is almost always bad.

Shifting Your Pattern of Focus

Most of us only see the world through one, or maybe two, perspectives. These perspectives are typically instilled in us through our childhood, our own experiences, or whoever spends the most time talking in our ears (news, religion, entertainment, etc.). The most important step in harnessing the power of your mind is the ability to see things in a different perspective — or shift your pattern of focus.

Remember, the subconscious mind likes to delete or hide things. Your next million-dollar idea or your life partner could be right in front of you, but you can't see it. Let me explain.

I want you to try to memorize the following number in the next ten seconds. I promise it's possible because I have taught thousands of people to do it.

Go ahead, set a timer, and see if you can do it.

132333435363738393

Now, there are going to be three types of people when looking at this number.

1. You have a photographic memory and memorize the number with no problem.

2. You spent a good five minutes trying to memorize the number and still are unsure if you memorized it correctly.

3. You didn't waste your time trying.

Unless you have a photographic memory, you probably struggled to memorize this number. That's expected. Our subconscious mind struggles to retain and process information past a few digits long. That's why we can memorize a four-digit pin or a name like "Jane," but if we need to memorize a phone number or a name with more than three syllables, we start to struggle.

Now, I want to show you what happens when you change your pattern of focus. What if, instead of a bunch of random numbers, you enabled your subconscious mind to see a pattern by breaking up the numbers into increments of tens?

13 – 23 – 33 – 43 – 53 – 63 – 73 – 83 – 93

Simply by changing your focus, you were able to make sense of these numbers and memorize them so much faster. That's the power of shifting your pattern of focus. Just by learning to do this, you will drastically change your life. Instead of focusing on the negative around you, start focusing on the positive.

Going through hard times does not make you depressed; choosing to focus only on the negative situations in your life makes you depressed. What if instead of focusing on the heartbreak, you were grateful that you were saved from a bad relationship.

Or what if instead of focusing on being fired, you focused on the opportunity to start a new career or business in a place that wants you to be there. Simply by being grateful and focusing on the good in your life, you will start to see a drastic change.

Apply This Now:

Step One:

Take a look at your patterns of focus. What's one thing that you find is holding yourself back from something you want? You have to be brutally honest with yourself. Do you have negative beliefs about making more money or how quickly you can reach the next level of your business? Maybe you have negative beliefs about finding true love or the perfect partner?

If you do, you need to trace that pattern back to its origin. What patterns were instilled in you during your theta stage that are now stuck? Maybe your dad taught you that money is bad, or you were cheated on several times, or you think you'll never be healthy because you were teased as a kid about your weight.

Step Two:

Once you get down to the root of the pattern, you need to ask yourself, *how can I reprogram this program of thought?* Reprogramming the thought simply means moving your focus from a negative pattern to a positive pattern. Other people have been cheated on but found true love. Other people have found the success you are looking to achieve — maybe you can too. Open your mind to these thoughts and allow yourself to see new opportunities. As you do this, you will start to see things that have been in front of you all along.

Step Three:

It's important to note that changing your pattern of focus does not *create* new opportunities and resources — it simply *reveals* them. When you view the world through the lens of limited resources and zero opportunities, what will you see? If you were able to view the world through the eyes or lens of a multi-millionaire or through a lens of endless opportunities, what would you see? Your mind always finds what you are looking for.

2

HOW ADOLF HITLER TURNED GERMANY INTO A KILLING MACHINE

Manipulating Emotions For Good

During World War II, Adolf Hitler managed to turn an entire nation into a killing machine. By tapping into people's innate tribal instincts, he was able to convince everyday people, like you and me, to turn on their neighbors, kill their friends, and betray their families. It is estimated that approximately six million Jews were killed by the Nazis during the Holocaust. Additionally, an estimated five to six million non-Jewish civilians, including people with disabilities, political opponents, homosexuals, and others deemed undesirable by the Nazi regime, were also killed in concentration camps and other mass killings. He didn't force people to do this. He didn't hold a gun to their head. People willingly followed him.

On the surface, his methods were simple. He used slogans, symbols, and public gatherings to sow seeds of fear and insecurity while also building an extreme feeling of pride and hope in the country. His goal was to make people so proud and hopeful for the future of their nation, make them feel as if they had been wronged...

Once this was achieved, he asked them to do the unthinkable.

The Three Concepts of Lebensraum

- The Need For Living Space

Physical Need: He was able to do this by repeating simple concepts until they were drilled into the German people's minds. The first was Lebensraum (translated as living space). He argued that Germany needed to expand its territory in order to provide room for its rapidly growing population. Of course, the only way to do this was to conquer the nations that surrounded them.

- A Superior Race

An Emotional Need: The second message was to emphasize the "superiority" of the Aryan race. This one took a bit longer, but by constantly reminding the German people of their superiority, he was eventually able to convince them to kill anyone that did not look like them or was not equal to their superiority.

- Mass Participation

A Sense of Belonging: To reinforce these concepts in the German people, Hitler and the Nazis held events that required everyone to participate. Anyone who did not openly participate or seem emotionally engaged at these mass events was identified and "dealt with" either by the crowd or by security personnel. You didn't even have to be resistant or cause a disturbance to be viewed as bad. You just had to not be emotionally involved. The result? A highly radicalized and submissive country that would do anything that their leader told them to do.

How was Hitler able to do this? How was he able to hijack nearly an entire nation and make them believe that killing millions of innocent people was okay? It was because he understood one extremely important principle. Humans aren't logical; they are emotional. If you want to gain authority over someone, you must learn to control their emotions.

Mastering Your Emotional Response

Imagine a world where you can't trust your own feelings and emotions, a world where your emotions can be easily manipulated by others. This is exactly what happened in Nazi Germany during World War II. Adolf Hitler and the Nazi party were able to tap into the emotions of the German people, playing on their feelings of national pride and resentment. They used this emotional manipulation to gain support for their hateful agenda, which led to the persecution and extermination of millions of innocent people.

Can you imagine the fear, the anger, the sense of betrayal that the German people must have felt as they were being subconsciously brainwashed by Hitler's rhetoric and propaganda? His speeches were designed to stir up strong emotions, to make people feel like they were part of something bigger than themselves, like they were part of a national movement. But in reality, he was just using them to accomplish his own evil desire.

The truth is that *all* of us are susceptible to this kind of manipulation. The ability to control and manipulate emotions is still being used to influence people every single day. Politicians and pastors use emotion to make you believe certain things. Salesmen and society use it to push us to take a certain action. At a more personal level, you may be making decisions in your life based on emotions that are keeping you from reaching the next level of success.

The reason this works so well is because the best persuaders don't lead with logic; they lead with emotions.

Emotions are the language of the mind.

If you want someone to change their belief, then you simply need to change how they feel about something — not how they see it. Sales is the perfect example of this. Imagine a brand-new salesperson who's been rejected by several potential clients. The first few times, it may hurt, but he can easily shrug off the feeling of rejection. By the hundredth call, it will be hard for him to push through the *emotions* of disappointment and frustration. This is why a lot of people quit when things get hard.

On the other hand, if the salesperson is able to change his emotional response to the rejection and focus on learning and finding the next opportunity to get a sale, he is far more likely to succeed in making a sale. No matter what your difficulty in life is, the easiest way to control your emotional response is to start shifting your focus. Here's how this works.

1. *Your mind receives data about your current situation.*

2. *Based on experiences and data, you create a perceived outcome.*

3. *Your mind then creates the emotion that will help achieve the perceived outcome.*

Let me share an example of how this works:

Imagine driving on a windy, curvy mountain road. The road is just wide enough for one car to pass and has no rails to keep you from plummeting to certain death.

If you are focused on the possibility of your car driving off the cliff, your focus shifts from seeing yourself enjoying the ride to dying or falling off a cliff — which then causes a stress response increasing the likelihood of it actually happening.

Your mind will tell you, *Oh no! We are going to drive off the cliff. Let's create an emotion that will help us do that.* The result is entering a manic state and suddenly you feel stressed. High blood pressure, less focus, sweaty palms — all of these biological responses will increase the likelihood of you either stopping the car or driving off of the cliff.

Here's the solution:

Rather than focusing on the worst-case scenario, you should train your mind to focus on your car making it to the end of the road. Imagine the beautiful view, the story you can tell, and the bliss of driving a sports car to the top of a mountain.

If you *focus* on these things, your emotions will be calm and focused, increasing your chance of staying on the road. When we stress about relationships, making more money, or failing at something, our mind automatically creates the emotions to achieve what we are focused on. Instead of becoming more productive, more focused, and more confident by focusing on the best-case scenario, we focus on the worst-case scenario and our mind then creates the very thing that we are trying to avoid.

Emotions are simply a strategy.

Overcoming Limiting Beliefs

Emotions control everything we do, but easily the greatest emotion that keeps us from achieving our goals is fear. Think of this question:

What is your biggest goal in life?

When you have an answer, I want you to ask yourself again with this one simple change. What is your biggest goal in life *if you knew you couldn't fail?* Most people will instantly change their answer to something far more impressive once we remove the idea of failure.

This question shows our underlying limiting beliefs. Between each of us and our ultimate satisfaction and happiness is a limiting belief that is usually based on fear. Fear of failure, fear of humiliation, fear of pain, fear of the unknown...the list goes on, but it all boils down to one thing. Fear.

In order to remove limiting beliefs from your life, you must learn to remove fear from your life. Ask yourself, *what caused you to be fearful?* Look back into your past and pinpoint the day that you started being fearful and ask yourself why. Once you have found this, you can literally hypnotize yourself to change that memory. What once gave you fear and held you back from your dreams, you can now use to create a powerful force for good.

Controlling Others Through Their Emotions

On August 26, 1939, Hitler addressed 20,000 people with one of his many famous speeches. Given as a rally cry as the country prepared to invade Poland, this speech was purposefully used to create the emotions needed to invade a country out of cold blood. First, he painted Poland as the instigator of the conflict. "The Polish state has refused the peaceful settlement of relations which I desired and has appealed to arms. Germans in Poland are persecuted with a bloody terror and are driven from their homes.

A series of violations of the frontier, intolerable to a great Power, prove that Poland is no longer willing to respect the frontier of the Reich." Although these statements were a complete lie, he was able to stir a sense of justice and anger by suggesting that Germans were being mistreated. His intention was clear; he wanted to conquer all of Europe, starting with Poland.

With his intention set, he was able to elicit the required emotions of pride, fear, and anger to persuade the German people to invade a peaceful country. With that emotion in place, he was able to suggest anything to his listeners and he did.

Not only did he push to attack Poland, but he also encouraged them to attack France and England and anyone else he deemed to be a danger to their country. Here are the words he used to push the entire world to war. "I am resolved to eliminate from the German territories the elements of the population which are harmful to us, just as we have already eliminated the Jews... I am firmly resolved to do battle, now that the hour has come, against France and England, and to destroy them before they can cross the seas to our Continent. We shall answer their attacks with poison gas."

Manipulating Emotions for Good

Let me be clear. Hitler was evil and his goals were evil. However, his understanding of emotions and how to persuade others to take action was pure genius. When you begin to gain control of your own emotions, you can start to apply the same lessons to other people. Here are the three main steps as mentioned above.

- *Have a Clear Intention*

For Hitler, this was conquering the world and killing entire people groups. Every speech he gave was with this in mind. The same mentality needs to be used in your life. Whether you're looking to close a deal, find a date, or land a new job — every action and every word you tell someone needs to have a specific intention in mind.

- *Elicit an Appropriate Emotional State* (excitement, sympathy, hope, despair, etc.)

Hitler knew that the only way to drive a nation to war was to pull on their heartstrings of patriotism and anger. Once that was done, convincing them to go to war was easy. Take a look at your next sales prospect, date, or major conversation — what emotion will be the most likely to get you your desired result. Pro tip: all emotions can get people to take action. It's important to know which action motivates each individual you talk to the most.

- *Anchor a Thought or Action to That Emotion*

Hitler knew that once he had created the emotion in his audience, they were primed for any suggestion. That's why he immediately went on to include that after invading Poland, they would invade France and England as well. Any time the German people thought of nationalism, of "living room," their thoughts would immediately be turned to attacking the rest of the world.

The lesson is this: once you learn to elicit an emotion, you can plant a thought in anyone's mind. Once you see someone extremely happy, sad, angry, or any strong emotion — be very careful of what you are planting in their mind.

It really is that simple. When you master these three simple steps, you can instantly gain massive authority in every situation you find yourself in. For most people, it takes months, years, or even a lifetime to master these results just in your own mind. In the next few chapters, I will show you how to master this in your own life and others in the next few days.

Apply This Now!

Step One: Take a look at the last time you were angry or hurt. How did you react afterward? Did the reaction help or hurt you? Now take a moment to imagine if you had controlled your emotional response. What would you have done differently? What emotional response would have helped you get the outcome that you wanted?

Step Two: Start to view your emotions as a strategy instead of a reaction. Think about a situation where you may find yourself feeling a strong emotion. Replace that emotion with one that will help you accomplish your desired goal instead of reacting to the initial feeling. For example, if you are in a fight and you feel angry and frustrated, what emotion will lead to a positive result if you replace the anger? It could be gratitude. Be grateful for the other person or the situation and allow that gratitude to guide you to a better, calmer solution.

Step Three: Take notes and keep track of your emotions and the results that they bring in different situations.

3

THE CIVIL WAR AND THE MORPHINE SHORTAGE

Placebo Effect and Achieving a Peak State

During the Civil War, nearly one million soldiers either died or sustained life-altering injuries. Due to a shortage of doctors and medical supplies, many soldiers spent their dying moments on a makeshift bed in an overcrowded hospital tent. Without doctors or medical supplies, they suffered from infection, untreated wounds, and poorly performed surgeries — there was very little that could be done.

That's why most soldiers wanted one thing. Morphine. Even if they knew they would lose a leg or possibly die in their sleep, at least morphine eased the pain while waiting for proper medical assistance. Of course, with so much pain and suffering, morphine was also in low supply. That's when doctors had to get creative.

Rather than delay surgeries until morphine arrived, doctors were known to mix morphine with water to help it last longer. And when that didn't work, they turned to hypnosis. Army surgeons would hypnotize injured soldiers before performing amputations. The results were dramatic, and to this day hypnosis still serves as an extremely effective form of anesthesia and even healing.

This is called the **Placebo Effect**. It is similar to placebo where a sugar pill or vitamin is given to a patient as a powerful medication. Hypnosis is such a powerful tool that dentist offices throughout the 1960s used to have a hypnotist in house to prepare their patients for painful procedures.

> *Personal Experience: I've seen this happen multiple times. The first time I saw hypnosis used in place of medication was when one of my clients came to me with a dilemma. She needed to have a root canal, but she is deathly allergic to anesthesia. She came to me as a last resort. Not only was I able to hypnotize her to feel no pain, she also was back on her feet the very next day with almost no pain, instead of experiencing the typical 2–3-day recovery period.*

The Nocebo Effect

Opposite of the placebo effect is the nocebo effect. Fabrizio
Benedetti is a neuroscientist and physician who devoted his life
to uncovering the secrets of the placebo and nocebo effects. His
work is largely based around understanding and explaining how
the placebo effect is more than just imagination but rather, a
complex dance between psychological, neurological, and physi-
ological elements. Furthermore, he has shown that placebos can
exert genuine, measurable influences on pain, anxiety, and other
symptoms.

Fabrizio's Mountain Top Experiment

In 2007, the Italy-based professor embarked on an experiment
to uncover the power of rumors in impacting human performance. His study centered around a group of students hik-
ing the Italian Alps to a height of 9,800 feet. To set the stage,
Benedetti whispered to one student about the possibility of thin
air causing excruciating migraine headaches. Like wildfire, this
rumor soon spread among the students, reaching more than a
quarter of the group by the day of the hike.

As the students ascended the mountain, those privy to the rumor began experiencing intense, migraine-like headaches. To
Benedetti's astonishment, their saliva analysis showed an am-
plified response to the low-oxygen conditions and an increased
presence of enzymes linked to altitude headaches. This intrigu-

ing discovery indicated that the subconscious mind's biochemistry had altered in the individuals affected by the rumor.

Benedetti's experiment had proven that negative expectations could be transmitted through social circles, rippling outward and causing nocebo effects in a vast number of subjects. It seems that simply witnessing another person in pain can amplify the experience of discomfort, suggesting that nocebo effects can silently transmit from one individual to another.

Self-Fulfilling Prophecies

Benedetti's experiment showed how simple it is for the mind to directly affect our body. All of his students were placed in the same environment, but because of preconceived notions, only twenty-five percent experienced severe negative responses. Your subconscious mind is the most powerful and intelligent tool in the world, but many of us never learn how to truly tap into its power. Again, this is because we tend to focus on the wrong things.

Out of the millions of things that we can focus on, people tend to hone in on the few negative things that are present in their life — and the mind automatically projects that negative situation into the future. Simply by focusing on the negative things in your life, you trap yourself in a cycle.

Negative state produces negative actions which produce negative results.

This is called a self-fulfilling prophecy. By focusing on the present negative, you take negative actions, which end up creating a negative future. This can look like asking yourself questions: What if I fail? What if they don't like me? What if this doesn't work out? What if I'm not rich enough, old enough, smart enough? When you feed your subconscious mind these thoughts, it makes sure that the future aligns with these thoughts. Your mind is so powerful that it will literally block all other outcomes simply based on what you feed it.

Warrior Monks

From the 11th to the 16th century, the monk warriors of Japan filled the hearts and minds of all who heard of them with both fear and awe. The primarily Buddhist monks were known for their incredible fighting abilities and their god-like speed and strength. Due to a decline in the political strength of Japan during that time, the monks formed their own military forces to protect their monasteries and communities from the attacks of warlords.

The monk warriors were trained from an early age to control their thoughts and emotions and to focus their minds on the task at hand. They practiced visualization, which involved mentally rehearsing their movements and techniques to achieve a level of automaticity and efficiency in battle. They also had a strict physical training regimen that emphasized strength, agility, and endurance.

Through years of discipline and mental training, the monk warriors achieved a level of focus and clarity that seemed almost supernatural. They were able to enter a state of "no-mind" where distractions and emotions did not affect them, and they were able to act with complete clarity and focus.

Their abilities were nothing short of astonishing.

They could break stones with their bare hands, resist arrows and sword strikes without flinching, and perform acrobatic feats that seemed impossible for humans. They were able to jump from tree to tree with incredible ease, move with such grace and speed that they appeared almost weightless, and climb walls and trees with such speed that they appeared to be defying gravity.

These seemingly supernatural powers were achieved by the monks' ability to enter and maintain a peak state. This state allowed them to block out all distractions and act with clarity and efficiency. They were able to enter a realm of existence where pain, fear, and chaos simply did not exist.

The monk warriors had a deep understanding of the power of peak state and the impact it could have on their abilities. By entering this state, they were able to perform feats that were simply beyond what others could do. Their ability to enter a peak state allowed them to instill fear in their enemies and inspire confidence in their allies.

Creating a Peak State In Your Life

Operating in a peak state will literally open your mind to new opportunities and give you the confidence to accomplish anything, as opposed to a negative state that will block you from opportunities and keep you from acting in your best interest.

Getting into a peak state can look different for a lot of people, but it normally involves some kind of outward expression that increases blood flow and releases positive hormones that can help you to think and act in a way that will lead to more positive daily outcomes and experiences. Here are four key components of operating in a peak state, followed by a way to change your thinking for the better:

- **Abundance Mindset:** Having an abundance mindset means that you focus on the abundance of resources available to you, instead of the scarcity of them. This alone will help you feel more confident and motivated as you go after your goals and dreams. It will also help you be more generous with your time and energy, leading to more positive interactions with others and a higher perceived authority.

- **Association:** The old cliché is true: you are the sum of the five people you associate with. It doesn't matter how strong your mindset or good intentions are; if you are surrounded by people who will whisper "rumors" and "negative prophecies" in your ear, you are holding yourself back. The key to operating in a peak state is removing all negativity from your life. Practicing gratitude is a great way to do this. By focusing on the things you have and not the things you don't have, you are able to reduce stress, clear your mind, and walk with more clarity and peace.

- **Action:** The last key of operating in a peak state is to take action. When you have increased blood flow, awareness, and positive hormones flowing, you instantly increase your confidence and ability to perform at a higher rate. That's when you need to take action. Not only will you have a higher success rate, especially in persuading others, but you will also reinforce in your mind that this mode of thinking is how you want to operate.

- **Rewarding Yourself:** The key with taking action when you are in a peak state is to reward yourself for entering this state. That way your mind will want to return. Essentially, you're training your mind to think, "Hey, when we get to a peak state, good things happen." This train of thought will carry you forward and continue to drive behaviors that increase your confidence and authority.

At the end of the day, operating in a peak state is all about changing your beliefs. Just like a negative mindset forces your subconscious mind to find negative outcomes in your life, the same applies to forcing yourself to be in a positive or peak state.

Emotions drive behavior, and your belief supports that emotion. So, by forcing yourself to enter a peak state, you will change the emotions that are driving your behavior. Eventually, you won't have to force yourself to do this. Putting yourself into a peak state is a skill and just like any skill, the more you use it, the easier it gets. In the next chapter, we will discuss how to shorten this process.

Personal Experience: In 2020, I had a client in distress over COVID-19. He called me in the middle of a panic attack because he was unsure how his business was going to survive in the middle of the pandemic restrictions. We had a quick 30-minute hypnosis session to get him into a peak state and just like that, he found the answers he needed. We formed a plan to pivot his business and in just sixty days, he was able to grow his business 10x by operating in this peak state.

Apply This Now!

Step One: Take a look at the last time you felt truly amazing. What led you to feel this way? What did you do? Did you accomplish something amazing, or did you feel an extreme ability to focus? This was a peak state. Go ahead and write down how you felt and what you accomplished.

Step Two: Now I want you to imagine how it would feel to have the ability to turn this on at any time. Take a breath, close your eyes, and focus on the feeling of being totally focused and undistracted and the amazing things you can accomplish when feeling this way. Don't open your eyes until you have a clear mental image of what this would look and feel like. When you do, open your eyes, and get to work.

4

GALINA KORZHOVA, THE CHARMING THIEF OF MOSCOW, RUSSIA

The Basis of Hypnosis

Galina Korzhova was a woman from a small town in southern Russia. She grew up in a humble home with her family, and despite the challenges she faced during her upbringing, she was determined to make something of herself. Her path would eventually lead her to a life of crime, but it was not one that anyone could have predicted.

Korzhova was always a gifted talker. She had a way with words that could charm almost anyone. This talent would become her greatest asset in the world of crime. It all started when she was working at a local grocery store. One day, a woman came in and tried to buy groceries with a fake credit card. Korzhova was suspicious, but instead of calling the police, she struck up a conversation with the woman.

Within minutes, the woman had opened up to Korzhova and revealed her entire story. She was a professional thief, and she had been robbing stores across the city for months. Korzhova was fascinated by this lifestyle, and she soon adopted it to escape her own difficult circumstances.

Korzhova started small, with shoplifting and petty theft. But she quickly realized that robbing banks was where the real money came from. However, she knew that she could never use force or violence to accomplish this goal. Instead, she turned to her gift of persuasion. She began to study the psychology of human behavior, looking for ways to tap into people's deepest desires and vulnerabilities.

It wasn't long before Korzhova had perfected her technique. She would often approach her targets on the street, pretending to be a kind stranger. She would offer to remove curses, heal their sick relatives, or give them advice on their personal problems. She knew that people were more likely to trust someone who seemed genuinely interested in their well-being. Once she had gained their trust, she would simply convince them to withdraw money from their bank accounts and give it to her.

One of her victims, a bank teller, shared her experience.

"After meeting her [Korzhova] in the street, I found myself reeled in by her charming words."

The next thing the teller knew, she was outside the state bank Sberbank on Communist Street in Volzhky, with a plastic bag filled with 30,000 euros, $20,000, and the rest in rubles, totaling 2.6 million rubles or $81,000. It wasn't until a few hours later that the teller realized what had happened and informed her bosses at the bank.

Korzhova was able to accomplish her robberies in a matter of minutes, without ever resorting to threats or signs of force. Her approach was so gentle and sophisticated that many of her victims didn't even realize that they had been robbed until hours later.

Despite her success, Korzhova knew that her life of crime could not go on forever. She eventually became the subject of a major police investigation, and it wasn't long before they had enough evidence to arrest her. As the investigation continued, the police uncovered evidence linking Korzhova to up to 30 additional bank robberies, leading the media to refer to her crime spree as a "grand tour" around the country.

She was sentenced to several years in prison, but her story had already captured the public's imagination. Korzhova's legacy lives on to this day. She is remembered as a master of persuasion, a woman who was able to use her charm and charisma to get what she wanted.

A Gentle Approach

Most of us won't ever rob a bank, but we may find ourselves in a position where we need to ethically persuade someone to do something they don't want to do. There is a lot to learn from how this woman got away with her impressive crime spree. The first thing is to notice her approach. Rather than coming in with threats and demands, she won her victims over with her gentle demeanor. Imagine her success rate if she went straight for the kill.

"Give me the money now!" She would have some success, but it would be limited. That aggressive approach would lead to people calling the police and an increase in armed guards at other banks. She most likely would have been caught much sooner.

Rather, she used a different approach. She didn't use threats and she didn't use firearms. She used the most powerful tool available to her — someone else's mind. Imagine if your next sales call was not a conversation between you and your potential client; instead, it was a conversation between your potential client and their own mind.

Rather than spending the entire conversation trying to convince them to work with you or buy your product, you simply have to take a few moments to tap into their subconscious mind and let their own thoughts, past experiences, and emotions close the deal for you. How much easier and faster would it be to close the deal? By learning to tap into someone else's mind, this is possible.

The Basics of Hypnosis

Hypnosis can be quite difficult to understand, so let's break it down into steps using the robbery example above. In this chapter, we will solely focus on learning how hypnosis works. We will do this for one reason: it's safer. Hypnosis is not something to be used casually. Before you start trying to hypnotize others, you need to make sure you understand what you are doing to someone. We will ensure that you don't misuse it while still learning how it works. Once you understand how it works, the best way to practice is on yourself. Remember: anything that you do to yourself, you can also do to others.

- **Step One: Frame Control**

Galina gained the attention of her victims (or partners, however, you view it) by luring them in with promises of healed loved ones, answered prayers, and other solutions to personal problems. Once she had their attention, she was able to plant her hypnotic suggestions.

This is called frame control or setting a frame. Setting a frame sets boundaries for your hypnotic experience. By establishing what you are about to do for someone, you help them to clear their mind and greatly increase the effectiveness of suggestion.

For you, this could look like this. Instead of telling a client that giving you money is a good investment, you might tell them that what you're about to share with them will make them very wealthy or that it will secure their legacy in history. Now, rather than focused on the idea of giving you money, their mind is drawn to the potential of wealth or fame. That's setting a frame.

Here are several keys to setting the perfect frame:

1. **Setting expectations:** *Establish the expectations for your self-hypnosis experience by framing it as a safe and positive experience. Remember, in self-hypnosis, you are in control and you are using it to make your life better.*

2. **Defining the problem:** *What is the problem you want to solve? Is it your relationship with money, fame, romantic partners, or a negative thought pattern? Your hypnosis session will be much more impactful if you have a clear problem defined that you are looking to address.*

3. **Shifting perspectives:** *Use frame control to shift your perspective and reframe your experiences and beliefs. Life doesn't happen at you; it happens for you. When you can view negative memories or events in this life, you will be able to find the positivity in the worst of your memories and situations.*

- **Step Two: Induction**

Once you've mastered setting a frame, you must take control of someone's mind. When Galina had caught the attention of her subject, her next step was putting them in a hypnotic state. If I had to guess, she probably did this through a conversational induction. By talking to her clients and drawing their mind into a relaxed, open state, she would be able to access their subconscious without them realizing what was happening. The key to a successful induction is getting someone to lower their guard. Oftentimes, the thing that is blocking us from our deepest desires is our conscious mind.

In a seminar setting or a performance setting, this can be done in many different ways, but the goal is the same — to put someone in a trance where they are more suggestible and open to change. Here are a few of the options for hypnosis.

Shock Induction:

If you've been to a hypnosis show or one of my seminars, you have seen this technique. It normally involves distracting the subject by throwing them off balance, shaking their hand or confusing them, and then telling them to "sleep!" You'll often see this from stage hypnotists because it is quick and entertaining to watch. The key here is that you are distracting the subject's conscious mind while speaking to their subconscious.

Conversational Induction:

Conversational inductions involve talking to an individual and mingling your hypnotic suggestions into the conversation. As I said earlier, my guess is that Galina used this method during her robbery spree. By arousing feelings of hope, sadness, and anger about their loved ones' problems, she was able to create a state where their mind was open to suggestion. This is accomplished through storytelling to create a relaxed state

or an even stealthier approach where you are embedding hypnotic suggestions directly into your conversation.

> *Personal Experience: I had a client that was very resistant to shock inductions. I quickly shifted to telling them a story about a farmer who was working extremely hard and found themselves exhausted by the end of the day. I then invited my client to imagine with me how tired the farmer must have felt. Within a few minutes, they were deep in trance and I was able to hypnotize them.*

Progressive relaxation

The easiest comparison for this is to do a guided meditation. This is similar to a conversational induction, but instead of storytelling, you are giving direct commands that lead to a relaxed state. *Close your eyes, relax your mind...your forehead, your chest...now sleep.*

There are many other types of inductions, but starting with these will give you a strong grasp of how to lead people into a hypnotic state.

- **Step Three: Planting a Suggestion**

"Go to your bank and put $20,000 inside of this bag. Once you've done that, you will bring it back to me and forget about everything that just happened." Again, I wasn't there, but Galina's suggestion may have looked something like this. A suggestion is the part of hypnosis where you start controlling and directing people's behavior.

And yes, it is exactly as dangerous as it sounds. The actual thoughts that you plant in someone's head can vary from changing a childhood belief to retraining how you relate to negative situations or it could be something darker such as telling someone to fall in love with you against their will or to unknowingly rob a bank and give you the money.

Disclaimer: I am not responsible for how you use this power, but I hope that you will use it for good.

The key to planting a good suggestion is to make it clear and precise. The mind responds best to simple messages.

As a life and business coach, I help people break out of limiting beliefs, learn new skills, and open their minds to new opportunities for their businesses. As a car salesman, you may sell them on the latest Aston Martin or Mercedes. As a CEO, you may suggest how investing in your company will be the best investment they ever made.

However, when you are hypnotizing yourself, this is when you will want to remove negative or limiting thoughts and replace them with new beliefs and thoughts and open your mind to new opportunities.

Whatever your goal is, it is important to make the suggestion as clear as possible. It should be a specific outcome tied to a strong emotion. For example, if your goal is to get someone to invest $500,000 in your company today, your suggestion could look like this:

Imagine investing your money and earning a good profit; how would you feel? Are you ready to do that?

That could work, but this would be better:

Imagine how ecstatic (strong emotion) you would feel if you invested $500,000 dollars and received a 45% return (specific outcome) in just three months. Are you ready to invest that money?

The same method should be used on yourself. Instead of saying.

I will earn a lot of money and get my company out of debt this year.

You should say:

In seven months, I will be relieved and peaceful(strong emotion) because I will have earned an extra $2,000,000(specific outcome) and my company will have erased its $450,276.31 of debt(specific outcome).

By following this simple blueprint, you'll dramatically change your life and find yourself achieving your goals much faster and with more consistency. You'll learn more about how to use suggestions later in the book, but this is a good start. Remember the key is to make your suggestions crystal clear: a specific outcome tied to a strong emotion.

- ### Step Four: Action

Hypnosis is not a magical solution. In order for it to work, the individual has to participate in the process and follow through on the suggestions given by the hypnotist. Once you have planted the suggestion in someone's mind, it's time to let them take action. It also makes it easier for you to re-hypnotize the subject. Taking action on hypnotic suggestions reinforces the hypnotic state, making it easier for the person to enter into hypnosis in the future and respond more readily to hypnotic suggestions.

Speed Is Critical

Most people take years to change a habit and that's after they have prolonged deciding to change. This is why many of us find ourselves stuck when we are trying to take our life to the next level. We think that delaying a decision is simply choosing to wait, but what it actually does is further affirm the current beliefs and thoughts that you have. In other words, you are digging yourself into an even bigger hole.

This cycle compounds until eventually, it seems impossible to break out of our circumstance. That's why speed matters. When you are ready to close a deal, start a new relationship, or take your life in a positive, new direction, speed is critical.

By learning to utilize hypnosis in your own life, you can move quickly. Bad habits can be broken in a few minutes; new habits can be installed in a matter of seconds. The more you begin to understand and use hypnosis in your life, the more you will literally be able to transform yourself in minutes.

5

GALINA KORZHOVA, THE CHARMING THIEF OF MOSCOW, RUSSIA (SPLIT)

Apply It Now!

Step One: Find a place where you can practice "hypnotizing someone." Have a clear goal in mind and go through the steps of hypnotizing. Set the frame of what you want them to do, then look to induce them with one of the steps above (shock, conversational, or relaxation). Once you have them listening and engaged, see if you can get them to follow your suggestion. It may feel awkward, but this is the best way to start learning. Make sure to record yourself!

Step Two: Watch the recording and critique. Did you set the frame well? Was your subject actually in a trance before you made the suggestion? Did they follow your direction?

Step Three: You'll want to keep doing this. Do it with friends, family, or even strangers. If possible, you always want to record so that you can critique yourself.

*Note: Your success will likely be fairly low the first few times. There is so much more to learn, but this process is necessary!

6

Sigmund Freud and the Oedipus Complex
Learning To Love Strangers

In the early 1900s, Sigmund Freud, a young Austrian doctor, was establishing himself as one of the early fathers of psychotherapy. One of Freud's most famous developments was the Oedipus Complex theory. Based on the Greek mythological story of Oedipus, this theory was instrumental in Freud's development and practice of psychoanalysis.

The story goes like this:

When Oedipus was born, his father, King Laius of Thebes, was told by an oracle that his own son would kill him. To prevent this prophecy from coming true, he ordered for his newborn son to be left to die on a mountain. However, a kind shepherd found the baby and gave him to King Polybus and Queen Merope of Corinth, who raised him as their own.

As Oedipus grew older, he became aware of a prophecy that he would kill his father and marry his mother. Terrified that the prophecy might come true, Oedipus left Corinth and set out for Thebes. On the way, he unknowingly killed King Laius, his father, in a dispute, thus fulfilling the prophecy. When Oedipus arrived in Thebes, he found that the city was plagued by a terrible monster called the Sphinx.

The Sphinx would ask riddles to anyone who passed by, and if they couldn't answer correctly, she would kill them. Oedipus was able to solve the Sphinx's riddle, and as a reward, he was made king of Thebes and was married to the widowed Queen Jocasta, his mother.

Years later, when a plague struck the city, Oedipus consulted an oracle to find out how to end it. He discovered that the only way to end the plague was to find and punish the killer of King Laius. Through his investigation, he came to realize that he was the killer, and that Jocasta was his mother and his wife. Overcome with shame and disgust, Jocasta killed herself, and Oedipus, horrified by his own actions, blinded himself and exiled himself from Thebes.

The Oedipus Complex Theory story

Freud saw the story of Oedipus as an example for the human psyche, where individuals are unconsciously driven by their desires, leading to tragic consequences. Based on this story, he formed the Oedipus Complex Theory. According to Freud,

The Oedipus Complex is a stage in a child's psychosexual development where they experience unconscious sexual desires toward their parent of the opposite sex and jealousy towards their same-sex parent.

Freud believed that the Oedipus complex was a natural and universal phenomenon and that it was present in all human beings. He saw it as a crucial stage in a child's development, as it helped them navigate their feelings of sexuality, aggression, and identity formation.

The story of Oedipus had a profound influence on Freud's thinking. He saw many parallels between Oedipus's story and the experiences of his patients. Like Oedipus, many of his patients were unconsciously driven by their desires for their opposite-sex parent and feelings of jealousy toward their same-sex parent.

Freud believed that many psychological symptoms were related to repressed sexual desires and unconscious thoughts and memories, and that by accessing the patient's subconscious through hypnosis and free association, he could help them work through these issues.

Freud used hypnosis to help people overcome their repressed desires. While you may not be helping people to overcome repressed sexual desires, you may need to understand that they have desires and thought patterns based on their childhood. By learning to mirror and read people, you will be able to gain

access to their mind and hypnotize them to think differently —
just like Freud.

Building Rapport

When building a relationship with someone, it's important to
make them feel understood and seen. The important thing to
remember is that most people are more similar to you than they
are different. If you can understand what bothers you and how
you react, you will find that others are the same. By connecting
the dots, you'll be able to connect to people much faster.

To figure out how others behave, you need to find out how they
think. *How does a person think about failure? Does the person
understand why they think or act a certain way? Are they open to
change?* It will be a very rare case that you can just ask someone
these questions and get an honest answer.

Most people aren't self-aware and asking these questions will
cause discomfort and cause them to be very guarded. This is the
exact opposite of what you need from someone when you are
building rapport. In order to get the answers to these questions,
you will need to use a stealthier approach. Here are three ways
to accomplish this based on the Oedipus and Electra Complex
Theories:

Examine Their Past

Examine someone's past to see how their upbringing and experiences are influencing their decision making today.

A person's past and upbringing are great tools to use when connecting with them and understanding their needs. For example, if a man does not relate well to his father, he probably hasn't sorted out his childhood problems and will most likely have resentment toward father or male authority figures.

He will probably be more comfortable with women and will veer away from things that are too masculine. In order to influence such a person, you will need to be sure that you steer clear of triggering the things that they hate. Don't talk in a deep authoritative tone, don't talk about your strong relationship with your father. If you do, you will greatly ruin your chances of building rapport.

Emulate Their Behavior

Once you understand someone's view of life and how their past affects them, you can begin to mirror their experiences. Be someone they can relate to. For example, you could say something like: "I understand what it's like to have (fill in the blank)" or "I know how it feels to (fill in the blank)." This could be anything from family issues, loss of loved ones, or growing up in a household that struggled to make ends meet. Connecting with someone over shared experiences is a powerful tool to build rapport.

Change Their Thinking

Help people overcome their past by showing them how to change their thinking. A great way of doing this is by explaining how you overcame similar experiences. For example: "I understand what you're feeling. I had similar experiences and feelings, but I have committed to not staying in that place. I have decided to move forward from (negative experience) to improve my life!"

Seeing that someone else was able to overcome their past will encourage them to adjust their thinking and adopt the same philosophy in their own life. It will also make them feel a connection to you as someone they can look up to and trust. Trust is everything.

Active Listening

Everything else that you will learn about building rapport is based on active listening, which means paying close attention to what the other person is saying and responding in a way that shows you understand and empathize with them. This leads to extremely advanced hypnosis techniques such as presuppositions, embedded commands, and strong suggestions. For starters, you will need to master the following active listening techniques that allow these more advanced techniques to work with a highly powerful effect.

Mirroring

Mirroring is a technique of subtly mimicking the other person's nonverbal cues, such as body language, tone of voice, and breathing patterns. This technique is effective because it makes the other person feel understood and creates a sense of similarity. Most people don't realize this, but the easiest way to picture how mirroring works is a family or group of friends that makes the same face when they are surprised, or they make similar gestures when talking. They may not even realize they are doing it. This is due to having years of rapport, you can quickly mimic this by paying attention when someone is talking.

Using these techniques can help you build rapport more quickly and allow the person to feel more comfortable sharing with you and listening to what you have to say.

Body Language

Chase Hughes, a good friend of mine and a master of persuasion, can discover a person's career, relationship status, mental state, eating disorders, job satisfaction, and other key points of their status simply through body language, hair, clothes, nails, skin tone, eyes — pretty much everything you can see on a person.

When he is in a conversation with someone, he is extremely attentive to both their verbal and non-verbal cues.

In a five-minute conversation, he will literally read hundreds of non-verbal cues in addition to what the person is verbally telling him. These cues provide him with extremely valuable information that helps him build rapport and trust very quickly with a person in just a few minutes of conversation.

Here are a few basics that will help you as you start to master reading body language.

Lines In Forehead: These mean a person is more agreeable. If you are looking to quickly persuade someone, you will want to look for lines in their forehead.

Here are two more advanced methods I learned from Chase.

Eyebrow Flashes: An easy way to test if someone is in rapport with you is by flashing your eyebrows. If they do it back, they are in rapport and more likely to accept suggestion.

Smooth Lower Eyelid: This means that someone is more suggestible and is more likely to have been in a cult. It's also important to note that successful people are more open minded and also more susceptible because they are always looking to learn and improve.

Breaking Rapport

Rapport is extremely fragile and can be broken in an instant. When it comes to building lasting connections with people, it's important to understand how your own behavior can affect those around you. In this regard, two extreme emotions that can have a powerful impact on your ability to connect with others are anger and extreme happiness. The most obvious way to break rapport is through anger.

When you're angry, your body language changes, your voice becomes louder, and you can sound harsh and aggressive. All of these changes will cause the person you're interacting with to feel threatened, become more defensive, and be less open to talking. When you lose control of your anger, you risk pushing others away and damaging any rapport you may have built with them.

Extreme happiness can actually have similar results. It might seem counterintuitive, but being excessively happy can also break rapport with others. When you sound overly exuberant, you can come across as insincere or even manic. Your tone may sound too high-pitched or forced, and your body language can become exaggerated.

All of these things will make the person you're interacting with feel uncomfortable or even intimidated. Especially while you are dealing with high status individuals, it may make it difficult for them to take you seriously. Whenever you approach someone, you want to seem authentic, mild-mannered, and relatable; this will make it much easier to build rapport quickly.

Personal Experience: I remember going out with a buddy of mine and his girlfriend. It was a high-class bar in L.A. and we were having a good time, but my friend noticed that his date was acting weird. He had no idea why she was acting that way, but there was something I noticed. Looking down, I saw that her feet were pointed away from my buddy while his feet were pointed at her. I followed her body language across the room and saw a guy whose feet were also pointed at my buddy's girl. I walked across the room and struck up a conversation with the guy.

"Hey, you come here a lot. Didn't you have a girlfriend then." The guy nodded. "Yeah, she's actually over there, but we aren't together anymore." I walked back to my friend and told him the situation. He tilted his head back knowingly and walked back to his date. "If my ex happened to be here and I was paying attention to her instead of you, how would you feel?" He had a smirk on his face as he finished. She caught the hint.

She was shocked that he even knew her ex was there or that she was making him jealous. She shook her head and snapped out of the mode. The rest of the night was very enjoyable for all of us, and her body language completely changed. Two things to note. One: by reading body language I was able to deduce what was causing the conflict. It had nothing to do with anything my buddy did. Two: my buddy exhibited extreme composure.

When he realized what was going on, he did not respond in an angry manner and destroy rapport with his girlfriend. He took

the information and calmly gave her an option: "Me or him."
This is how you can start to apply the things that you learned in
this chapter. Imagine how it would work in a business meeting
or your own relationship. Simply by reading the body language
and the rest of the room, you can remove negative energy and
distractions and close a deal.

Apply It Now!

Step One: Go somewhere where you can meet a stranger with some time to talk. Set a goal to establish rapport within five minutes or less. Practice mirroring their body language and verbal cues. Take time to note how they move and talk, and make sure to find common ground to build a connection.

Step Two: Test your rapport by asking them to do something out of the ordinary. This could be getting a number from the opposite sex, having them buy you a small item, or holding your hand. Have fun with this. If you can't push past the stranger boundary, you haven't successfully built rapport.

Step Three: If you were not able to build a strong rapport with someone, you need to analyze the reason. Did you have rapport and then break it with an extreme emotion or action? Did you mirror them? Did you build similar interests? Were you clear with your intention and specific with your language? If not, take notes on how you could improve.

7

BENNY HINN – FAITH HEALER

Eliciting an Emotional Response

100 million dollars. That's how much televangelist and faith healer Benny Hinn makes every year by healing people around the world. Although his healing career began much earlier, he came to prominence in the 90s when his program, "This Is Your Day" was aired daily on the Christian TV Network. The years that followed were full of televised healings from around the world. One of the most notable healings was when he healed one of the few boxers to defeat Mike Tyson.

In 1994, boxing champion Evander Holyfield stood in front of a crowd who had gathered to witness the miracles of televangelist Benny Hinn. Before Hinn and the crowd, Holyfield begged for God's healing. He had just been diagnosed with a condition in which the left ventricle of his heart could not work properly and so his blood struggled to pump. To add to his desperate situation, this medical condition was revealed just before he was supposed to fight the biggest opponent of his life — Mike Tyson.

A wave of Hinn's hand did what countless heavyweights had been unable to do and knocked Holyfield to the ground. Holyfield reported a warm feeling flooding his chest as he collapsed. As Holyfield lay on the stage, Benny Hinn turned to the crowd.

"The Lord is telling me now: he is repairing Holyfield's heart completely."

When Holyfield returned to the doctors, his heart was indeed pumping once more. Although doctors reported that he'd been misdiagnosed, Holyfield credited no one but Benny Hinn for his return to the ring.

Holyfield was so thrilled that he even agreed to write Hinn a check for $265,000, needed, as Hinn told him, to "underwrite the costs of the crusade." Later that year, Holyfield would also go on to defeat Mike Tyson.

Healings such as this one led Benny Hinn to build a massive following and host packed events wherever he goes. With millions tuning in to watch his healing sessions on TV and the internet, he has established himself as a prominent figure in today's society.

Despite the success, not everyone believes that Benny Hinn is truly healing people.

For me the question is not about the legitimacy of people being healed or Hinn's tax payment behaviors. I have no reason to doubt that there is any issue with those things. For me, the question is simply this: *Is this miraculous performance some kind of supernatural or magical occurrence or is it simply based on the power of suggestion?*

Eliciting Emotion

Whether you are religious or not, it is hard to ignore the work that Benny Hinn has claimed to do. As a hypnotist, I believe that it is possible to perform these miracles. I've done it myself and I know that with proper training, others can do it as well. With that being said, I am aware that there may be some people who view my own events as some kind of magic trick or some supernatural intervention, *but it's truly just hypnosis.*

However, with millions from around the world claiming to be healed through his work, it's worth taking a look at his techniques and methods. The first thing to note is his use of eliciting emotions. In order to get someone to take action, you need them to feel something. Hinn's events and even his entire brand are designed to create an emotional response.

The music, the laying of hands, and dramatic waving of hands is all used to create emotion — which leads people to be in a highly suggestible state. Perfect conditions for a 'supernatural' healing. In order to successfully create a state of elicit emotion, you must master the concept of emotional strategy. Here are the basics.

Emotions Create Motion

Positive emotions move you toward something. Negative emotions move you away from something.

Understanding how to leverage positive and negative emotions is an extremely powerful way to influence people's behavior. The basic idea is to learn which emotional response is needed to motivate someone to take a certain action and how to intentionally create that emotion.

On the positive side, you can use emotions like happiness, joy, and excitement to encourage people to take positive actions. This is most commonly seen in sales. If you're trying to get someone to buy a product, you might show them how happy and fulfilled they'll be once they own it. This positive emotion can create a desire to take action and make a purchase.

On the other hand, you can use negative emotions like fear, anger, and guilt to motivate people. For example, if you're trying to convince someone to quit smoking, you might show them images of diseased lungs or tell them about the health risks associated with smoking.

This negative emotion can create a sense of urgency and a desire to take action to avoid the negative consequences. It's important to note that using negative emotions can be risky and even unethical if done in a manipulative way. It's important to use these emotions in a way that is honest, respectful, and ultimately beneficial for the person you are trying to influence.

While most people are usually motivated by positive emotions, it's important to note that both positive and negative emotions are effective in moving people to take action. It just depends on the individual and what they respond to. The bottom line is this:

By learning to elicit an emotional response, you bypass a person's rational thinking, which makes it much easier to persuade them to take action or change their beliefs.

Storytelling

One of the most common ways to create a state of elicit emotion is to use language and imagery that triggers strong emotional response. This might involve telling a story that evokes empathy by using vivid and descriptive language or could be as simple as using a few sentences to create an emotional response. Pictures and videos are a great way to do this as well.

For example, in the case of Benny Hinn, he needed to stir up a strong sense of hope and expectancy from his followers. By telling stories of people he had healed and using descriptive language to paint a vivid picture of someone's suffering, he was, and still is, able to connect to the desires of his audience. While telling these stories, he and his team would scan the crowd for someone that is in rapport with him. Nodding heads, a steady gaze, and other nonverbal cues will show who is in rapport.

Storytelling is part of the induction phase of hypnosis. In order for it to be powerful, it needs to be three things:

Relatable, Emotional, and Specific.

A good hypnotic story will be relatable to your subject. They will be able to put themselves in the story because the story speaks to a pain or a problem that they have been through or are currently going through. It will be emotional because it is either pushing toward or away from something.

And it will be specific — you need them to feel a specific emotion that encourages a specific emotion. For Hinn, he pushes people to believe that he is capable of healing them. For you, it could be pushing someone to believe that you are the best investment option for them or that you are the best person to be in a relationship with

Personal Experience: At one of my seminars, I had a man on stage who wanted to quit smoking. He knew it was hurting him, but nothing had worked to help him change. In order to create a negative emotion around the action of smoking, I planted the thought in his head that cigarettes were the most disgusting tasting thing he had ever tasted

*in his life. I then instructed him to light a ciga-
rette and take a smoke. It was impossible for him
to do it. Imagine trying to purposely put something terrible and rotten in your mouth — your
mind won't let you do it. That's because there is
a negative emotion of disgust associated with the
outcome of tasting that disgusting thing. This can
also happen if we have a negative emotion toward
relationships, making more money, or even going
to the gym. The easy fix is to hypnotize yourself
to focus on the potential positive outcome of taking
action.*

Social Pressure and Thinking Outside the Box

Sometimes, it isn't possible to connect your situation directly to
a story, or you need to move with a stronger sense of urgency. In
a situation like this, you will need to think outside the box when
eliciting emotion. The goal is still the same, but you are doing it
in a roundabout way. For example, if you are struggling to create
rapport with someone, instead of spending more time creating
rapport, you may need to create a sense of duty or urgency for
someone to act.

The easiest way to think of this is telling an employee that you
need to speak to a manager. Have you ever been at a restaurant

where you never got your drinks, your server had a terrible attitude, and your order was completely messed up? After all that, the server brings you the bill for the food without any apology or discount. Most likely, you will ask to speak to the manager. When this happens, two things will happen.

Either the server will change his demeanor and instantly become more accommodating, or he keeps his attitude, you get a discount, and he risks losing his job. This is a form of social pressure. The reason that the server wasn't giving you good service is because they didn't view you as an authority. By turning to their authority (the manager), you are able to elicit an emotion of fear or respect to get the desired outcome that you had.

Another indirect way of doing this is thinking outside the box. This is important when you are asking someone to do something that requires them to stretch the rules a bit or take immediate action. For this method, you need to ask yourself the question:

What situation would make this behavior okay?

Speeding to get your pregnant wife to the hospital, skipping a line because your kid is sick, or skipping protocol to help someone in danger are great examples of how this can play out.

At the end of the day, you need to remember this: *everyone responds to emotions*. Most people respond better to positive emotions; others respond to negative emotions. By understanding which emotions drive them, you are able to elicit that emotion and gain incredible authority and persuasion over everyone you meet.

Apply It Now!

Step One: Earlier in the book, I asked you to examine your own emotional response to different situations. Now, you need to examine how to create an emotion in others. Take a moment to think of the last time you had a fight with someone. What was their emotion? Were they happy, sad, defensive, calm? What was the result of their emotion?

Step Two: Ask yourself, *what emotion did I need that person to feel to have a good result in that situation?* Now think of ways that you could've elicited that emotion in that moment. Maybe a hug, a joke, an apology. Think of the best response that would have created an emotion that allowed the person to be receptive to your words.

8

MARTY HOMLISH AND SAP, EARLY 2000s

How You Say It Matters

In the early 2000s, SAP, a German software company, was struggling to sell its enterprise software to the American market. Despite its success in Europe, American companies were skeptical of SAP's product and were reluctant to switch from the software they were already using.

To address this challenge, SAP hired Marty Homlish as their new head of marketing. Marty Homlish was, and still is, a highly accomplished marketing professional. For several decades, he has been the front of leading companies such as Sony, SAP, and HP. After studying the company's product and marketing efforts, Homlish found the problem. SAP needed to change the language they were using to sell their software to the American market.

He recognized that the words the company was currently using was deterring American companies from buying SAP's product. There was nothing wrong with the product — just the language they used to describe it.

The first step in solving the language problem was shifting the focus from technical features to benefits: Homlish recognized that American decision-makers were more interested in the practical applications of software than its technical features. So, he shifted SAP's messaging to focus on the benefits of its software.

For example, instead of emphasizing the technical specifications of SAP's software, Homlish talked about how it could help companies improve their supply chain management, reduce their operating costs, and increase their productivity.

However, Homlish didn't stop there. He knew that the language he used to communicate SAP's value proposition needed to be exact and precise. He recognized that using vague or overly technical language could cause confusion or misunderstandings, which could ultimately derail SAP's efforts to win American customers. To overcome this, Homlish spent time studying how American executives talked about technology and business processes.

He analyzed the specific words and phrases they used and incorporated this language into SAP's messaging. For example, instead of using technical jargon, Homlish used everyday language to explain SAP's software. He used phrases like "streamline your operations," "reduce your costs," and "improve your bottom line" — all of which were familiar phrases to American decision-makers.

Homlish also recognized the importance of starting conversations with a clear goal in mind. He knew that building relationships with key decision-makers at target companies was crucial to SAP's success. To do this, he launched a series of executive dinners, where SAP executives would invite key decision-makers to dine with them in an intimate setting.

At these executive dinners, Homlish made a point of listening carefully to the concerns and challenges of the executives he was dining with and would tailor his language accordingly. For example, if an executive was concerned about the complexity of SAP's software, Homlish might use language that emphasized its ease of use and user-friendliness. Or, if an executive was concerned about the cost of SAP's software, Homlish might use language that emphasized its ability to save companies money in the long run.

Thanks to Homlish's language-based approach, SAP was able to turn its fortunes around in the American market. The company began to win major contracts with key companies such as Coca-Cola and Procter & Gamble. In just a few years, SAP's revenues in the American market grew from $500 million to $2.5 billion.

Understanding How People Talk

When you're trying to influence others, it's important to understand who you're speaking to. This means paying attention to their communication style, the language they use, and what's important to them.

How you say it is equally, if not more important than what you say.

To do this effectively, start by observing how the person you're trying to influence communicates. What words and phrases do they use? Are they more formal or informal in their speech? Do they prefer a direct approach or more indirect? This information can help you tailor your language to better resonate with them.

Additionally, it's important to understand the values of the person you're speaking to. What are their goals and priorities? What challenges are they facing? What motivates them? This information can help you craft a message that speaks directly to their needs and concerns.

Once you've gathered this information, you can start tailoring your messaging to be more effective. For example, if you're trying to persuade a potential customer to buy your product, you might use language that addresses their specific concerns and needs. Or, if you're trying to convince an investor to support your idea, knowing the words he uses and his motivation for investing will be extremely powerful.

Maybe he has a family he wants to provide generational wealth for or he likes to be associated with powerful brands. Knowing this will help you use language that speaks directly to his priorities and motivations.

Use Your Words to Prime People

When you speak, be specific with the words you say. Before you even ask for something, your words should prime their mind to respond to your request. You can accomplish this in two ways.

1. **Be Intentional:** Don't speak unless there is an intention behind your words. When you limit the words you say, you will instantly become more powerful.

2. **Define Your Outcome:** Maybe you aren't looking to land a date or drive a sale on the first conversation, but you need to have a clear outcome. Maybe you are speaking to build rapport or to read someone's emotional response. By guiding each and every conversation to a specific outcome, you will find yourself speaking with more persuasion and confidence.

3. **Use Strong and Assertive Language:** Using strong, active verbs will help exude confidence and a greater sense of authority. For example, instead of saying, "I

think that we should do this to improve your sales," say, "Doing this will increase your sales."

Tonality

Start paying attention to the advertisements you see and hear around you to observe better use of tonality. A car commercial might use a fast, energetic tone of voice to convey the thrill of driving the car. A clothing brand might use a sultry, seductive tone of voice to suggest that wearing their clothes will make you more attractive. Tonality refers to the way we say things, including our pitch, speed, and inflection. By varying these aspects of our speech, we can convey different meanings and emotions.

In personal relationships, tonality can also be a powerful tool for persuasion. For example, if you want to convince someone to do something, you might use a calm, reasonable tone of voice to make your case. Alternatively, you might use an excited, enthusiastic tone of voice to get them excited about your idea.

A slow, soothing tone of voice is extremely powerful in helping someone to relax and enter a trance state. Alternatively, use a more forceful tone of voice to suggest a behavior change, such as quitting smoking or losing weight. By varying your tonality, you can elicit different emotions.

Presuppositions

Presuppositions are assumptions that are taken for granted or implied within a statement. They are often used in language to influence people without them even realizing it. When used skillfully, presuppositions can be a powerful tool to influence people's thoughts and actions. For example, as a hypnotist I have told many clients something like this:

"As you begin to relax more deeply, you may start to notice your eyes becoming heavier and heavier."

This statement presupposes that the listener will begin to relax and that their eyes will become heavier.

Politicians use presuppositions to influence voters. For example, a political candidate might say, "When I am elected, I will lower taxes for middle-class families." This statement presupposes that the candidate will be elected and that they will lower taxes.

By making these assumptions, the candidate is more likely to win over middle-class voters — even if the voter knows that it most likely won't happen. A double bind is a kind of presupposition that is extremely valuable in closing a person to the decision you want them to make.

Rather than asking for a yes or no answer, you give the option of two positive answers. It looks like this. *Do you want to go on a date Thursday night or Friday night?*

Become Your Own God Through Your Words

God spoke the world into existence.

"Then God said, 'Let us make mankind in our image, in our likeness, so that they may rule over the fish in the sea and the birds in the sky, over the livestock and all the wild animals, and over all the creatures that move along the ground.' So, God created mankind in his own image in the image of God he created them; male and female he created them." Of all the actions that could be used to explain the beginning of time, the Bible shows us that it was God's *words* that brought the world into existence.

His words were what created everything around us, and he made us in his image. If his words were that powerful and we are made like him, then that means you have the ability *to speak things into existence.*

When you start to master the use of language, you will gain even more authority in your life. Most people don't understand how to use words or don't think that words are extremely important. This is wrong.

The words you use, at the least, show your expertise, confidence, and credibility. When used to their maximum power, words can alter thoughts and behaviors in people's minds and create a brand-new reality for yourself and those around you.

That's why you should view *every word you speak as a suggestion.*

Apply It Now!

Step One: Think about your last conversation. What was the purpose of your conversation? Did you build rapport, close a deal, or gain an understanding of the person you were speaking with? Take notes and look to adjust for your next conversation.

Step Two: The next time you talk to someone, be clear with your intention. No conversation should just be a casual conversation. You should always have a purpose. Take note of your conversation. Did your conversation stray from your intention? Were you able to control the outcome of the conversation through your words? Notice if you used specific and assertive language or more passive and general.

Step Three: Repeat. Once you start doing this, you will find it easier to have purposeful and connecting conversations. It may feel strange, but in the end, you will find yourself wasting less time and building stronger and more meaningful connections.

9

THE US MILITARY IN VIETNAM

How to Create Authority

During the Vietnam War, the US military faced a significant problem: soldiers weren't shooting the enemy. The military found that soldiers were often reluctant to fire their weapons, even in situations where their lives were in danger. This was a significant problem, as it meant that soldiers were not able to effectively engage the enemy, and it put their own lives and the lives of their comrades at risk.

To address this problem, the military embarked on a program of reconditioning soldiers to be more willing to use their weapons in combat. This program involved a variety of methods, including desensitization and exposure therapy.

Desensitization involved exposing soldiers to the sights and sounds of combat in a controlled environment, such as a firing range. This allowed soldiers to become more accustomed to the sights and sounds of battle and helped to reduce their anxiety and fear.

Exposure therapy involved gradually exposing soldiers to the stress and trauma of combat through simulated combat scenarios and other training exercises. This allowed soldiers to become more comfortable with the chaos and unpredictability of combat and helped them to develop the skills and confidence they needed to engage the enemy effectively.

The military also employed a range of psychological techniques to help soldiers overcome their reluctance to fire their weapons. These included propaganda and other forms of messaging that emphasized the importance of the mission, the need to protect their fellow soldiers, and the moral and ethical justifications for their actions.

Probably the most controversial method of training soldiers was conditioning soldiers to the idea of shooting their enemy. Drill sergeants were instructed to use language that taught the soldiers to hate the enemy. Images of Vietnamese soldiers were used in shooting practice and racial slurs were prevalent.

By the end of boot camp, soldiers had a completely dehumanized view of the enemy they were going to fight.

Ultimately, the military was successful in reconditioning soldiers to be more willing to fire their weapons in combat. This allowed them to engage the enemy more effectively and ultimately contributed to the success of the US military in the Vietnam War.

However, the reconditioning program also raised ethical and moral questions about the use of psychological techniques to manipulate soldiers and change their behavior.

Building Basic Obedience

The process of building obedience and discipline in soldiers is a critical aspect of military training. Countries and militaries around the world employ a variety of programs, repetitions, and other training methods to instill obedience and create a cohesive and effective fighting force.

One of the key ways that countries build obedience in their soldiers is through basic training, which is the initial phase of military training. Basic training is designed to transform civilians into soldiers, and it involves a rigorous program of physical and mental training. The training is designed to break down the individual and build them up into a cohesive unit that follows orders without question.

Basic training is often conducted in an intense and controlled environment where soldiers are subjected to strict discipline and repetition of tasks until they become second nature. The government spends a fortune on developing these programs because they recognize how important it is to have absolute authority over their soldiers.

The goal of the military in basic training is to turn off the "no" switch in a soldier's brain. When it comes to authority and persuasion, your goal should be the same. For example, before asking someone for the big ask, you need to establish a pattern of obedience. This is also called a "yes-set" pattern. This involves asking a series of questions that the listener will naturally answer "yes" to. This primes the subconscious mind to be more receptive to your suggestions.

> *Creating a yes-set pattern primes the subconscious*
> *mind to be more receptive to your suggestions.*

People that are dating do this all the time. Once you meet someone, you pretty much have an idea of whether you want to be with them or not. However, it's typical to have a few 'friend' dates, then asking someone to officially date you, then you ask for them to marry you.

Finally, you commit to them fully. This may seem like quite the romantic thing to do, but it's really more practical and psychological. Imagine if you met a stranger and the very first thing you asked is if they wanted to marry you. The answer would probably be no because you've built no trust or pattern of obedience.

Repetition Is Extremely Important

In order to solve the Vietnam Syndrome, the military realized that soldiers needed to go through the repetition of killing men. During basic training, tasks become automatic and ingrained in the soldiers' muscle memory. The problem was that soldiers were being trained to shoot guns, fight, and march in formation — but not in killing soldiers. To solve this problem, the military made a simple change — they changed the targets that the soldiers shot thousands of rounds at in training to look like a Vietnamese soldier.

This change had staggering results. During the Second World War, it was revealed that only about 20% of the men who fought in combat in Europe fired at an exposed enemy. Instead, they simply fired at nothing. By the end of the Vietnam War, that number had increased in the US Army to 90%.

In order to establish authority and obedience with others, you need to have the same process of repetition in your life and in others. Get people accustomed to doing business with you; get them used to coming to you to solve their problems; get them accustomed to seeing you everywhere. As you can already see, this is easily applicable in life and in business.

Marketing statistics tell us that it takes most people seven to eight exposures to a brand or product before they decide to buy a product. One ad won't do it; you often need more. However, there is a strong caveat to this statistic.

The reason that it takes people so many exposures to something before they will take action is that they don't trust the brand or product yet. That's why it's important for you to build trust with others as quickly as possible. Whether you're on social media, at a networking event, or anything, everything you do and say should be geared to build the perception of authority with those around you.

Speed Is the Difference Between Life or Death

Speed is a critical factor in establishing authority and achieving your goals. Imagine if the army had taken forty years to develop a system where soldiers were able to act effectively. We would've been sending soldiers into battle to die without ever firing their weapon. Whether you agree with war or not, that would be a disaster. Speed is equally important when you are looking to establish authority in your own life.

When you're able to move quickly to capitalize on opportunities or address challenges, you can demonstrate your competence and effectiveness and build credibility with those around you.

Speed is also a powerful tool for persuasion. The ability to quickly establish authority and rapport with some will have a direct effect on your ability to make money, create lasting relationships, and accomplish your dreams. Remember that your goals, no matter how big or small, will always be executed through others. Once you have authority and rapport, you need to quickly move to suggestion.

Overall, speed is crucial for taking control of your life. When you're able to move quickly, establish rapport and authority with people in a few minutes versus several months, you will find yourself accomplishing your goals and building influence at a rate faster than you may have imagined.

Propaganda and Power

I'm a patriot, and I think people should have some form of loyalty to their country, but I recognize that all countries are dedicated to subconsciously brainwashing their citizens. Soldiers understand this best. The whole point of boot camp is to erase your identity and get you to follow authority. You don't have to go to boot camp to experience – they do it in schools no matter what country you live in.

Growing up, I was taught American History. Basically, they taught me that America was the ultimate authority. Many of us are taught this about God as well. If you're religious, the same thing is true. Your pastors, imams, rabbis, or priests teach you to obey the authority of themselves, your holy Book and God – and in the process – they attempt to recreate you in their image. While most religions teach us to be better people, you have to be aware of who you are giving the power in your life.

Apply It Now:

1. Before you look at conditioning others to follow you, you need to self-reflect. Are you blindly following others? *hint: everyone follows somebody.* Determine who you are following and ask yourself this question: *What process did this person use to condition me to follow them?*

2. Start taking note of the things you do because you are following someone's lead. Are these things you want to do? do they line up with your personal goals? If not, it's time to start reconditioning yourself.

3. When you've done that work in yourself, start looking to others. What things can you do to start conditioning people to listen to you? *Hint: this is as easy as creating a yes-set pattern. How can you get people to start saying yes to you before leading them to the big ask?*

10

James Fitzgerald and The Unabomber

Using Patterns to Your Advantage

I n the early 1980s, a series of bombs began exploding across the United States. The targets were universities, airports, and other public places, and the bombs were often sent through the mail. The perpetrator was a mysterious figure who went by the name "The Unabomber."

Over the years, the Unabomber sent a series of letters and manifestos to the media, detailing his motivations and demands. He claimed to be a freedom fighter, fighting against what he saw as the oppressive forces of modern technology and industrial society. The letters were filled with misspellings, grammatical errors, and unusual punctuation, and they had a distinctive, rambling style.

Despite a massive investigation involving the FBI and other law enforcement agencies, the Unabomber remained at large. He continued to strike at random intervals, killing two people and injuring dozens more.

In the mid-1990s, the case was assigned to a young FBI agent named James Fitzgerald. Fitzgerald had a background in linguistics, and he was tasked with analyzing the Unabomber's letters to try and identify any patterns or identifying features.

At first, Fitzgerald found the task daunting. The Unabomber's letters were long, meandering, and often nonsensical. But as he began to analyze them more closely, he started to notice patterns and features that he could use to create a psychological profile of the bomber.

One of the most striking features of the Unabomber's writing was his use of language. He misspelled common words, used unusual grammar, and often used punctuation in unexpected ways. For example, he frequently used the word "that" in place of "who" when referring to people, and he often used a semicolon to separate clauses where a period or a comma would be more typical.

Fitzgerald also noticed that the Unabomber frequently used certain words and phrases in his letters. For example, he often referred to himself as a "freedom fighter" and used the phrase "the system" to describe the forces he was fighting against. He also used the word "KFC" to refer to Kentucky Fried Chicken, a term that seemed to have no obvious connection to his other writings.

Using these patterns and other features, Fitzgerald began to build a psychological profile of the Unabomber. He concluded that the bomber was likely a white male with a military background, who was angry at the government and had a grudge against universities. He also identified several distinctive words and phrases that the bomber used repeatedly in his letters.

Using this profile, Fitzgerald and his team began to narrow down their list of suspects. They eventually focused on a man named Ted Kaczynski, a reclusive former professor who lived in a remote cabin in Montana. Kaczynski fit the profile in several key ways: he was a white male with a military background, he had a grudge against universities, and he used many of the distinctive words and phrases that the bomber had used in his letters.

Fitzgerald and his team eventually obtained a search warrant for Kaczynski's cabin. They found a wealth of evidence linking Kaczynski to the bombings, including bomb-making materials, handwritten notes, and a copy of his infamous manifesto.

Kaczynski was arrested in 1996 and eventually confessed to the bombings. He was sentenced to life in prison without parole.

How Patterns Affect You In Life

One of the most powerful tools you can use in predicting behavior is pattern recognition. Nonverbal cues such as facial expressions, posture, and gestures can provide valuable insight
into a person's thoughts and feelings. Someone who is confident and self-assured might stand tall and make eye contact,
while someone who is anxious or uncertain might hunch their
shoulders and avoid eye contact. If a client is crossing their
arms, it may indicate that they are feeling defensive or closed off.
By identifying these patterns, you can adjust your approach to
better connect with your client and build trust.

Patterns and Personal Grooming

Historically, long hair and beards have been associated with
masculinity and power, particularly in male-dominated societies. In these societies, men who were seen as strong and powerful often wore their hair long and grew beards as a symbol
of their status and authority. This tradition has continued in
many parts of the world, and even in modern times, long hair
and beards are often associated with power and prestige.

However, the relationship between personal grooming and status is not always straightforward. In some cultures, long hair
and beards may be associated with rebellion or nonconformity,
and individuals who challenge social norms may choose to wear
their hair long or grow a beard as a form of self-expression.

In these cases, the symbolism of long hair or a beard may be more closely tied to individuality and nonconformity than to traditional power structures.

The way we present ourselves to the world can say a lot about who we are. Take note of how people present themselves, including their clothing, hair, and makeup. If they always wear formal clothing, it may suggest that they value professionalism and structure. By understanding these patterns, you can create a more personalized and effective hypnosis experience. If someone has a tattoo or piercing, they might be signaling a desire to be seen as more edgy or unconventional.

If someone has a consistent haircut, they probably work with people in a professional capacity. Oppositely, someone who doesn't spend time around people will typically show less concern with their image.

It is important to note that these patterns are not absolute and that individuals may behave differently in different situations or with different people.

However, by observing patterns in behavior, we can begin to make predictions about how individuals are likely to behave in a given situation. This can be useful in a variety of contexts, from personal relationships to business interactions.

Using Patterns to Persuade and Influence Others

Understanding patterns takes time, but the sooner you start, the sooner you will start seeing the world in a completely different way. By chunking data and comparing the present actions of others versus your previous experiences, you can start to predict the behaviors of others very quickly. By no means will you become an expert overnight, but you can start using people's patterns to your advantage by following these basic steps.

- **Step One: Sensory Acuity (Start Paying Attention)**

Sensory acuity refers to the ability to observe and interpret non-verbal cues, including body language, facial expressions, habits, tone of voice, and other subtle signals that convey emotions and thoughts.

- **Step Two: Create a Baseline**

Once you start becoming more acute to how people react and act, you can create a baseline. Imagine if your partner has woken up at 8:00 for the last two years, but they suddenly start waking up consistently at 8:15. That's a change, and you know that something has shifted. It could be something small or massive, but without establishing a baseline, you won't be alerted to the signs that something has changed. This could be the same for gym habits, response to stress, eating habits, etc.

- **Step Three: Find the Cause**

If someone is in a relationship with you and out of nowhere you see a massive shift in their behavior, something big has happened. Maybe they heard something about you, maybe they feel like they are losing you, or maybe they're having an affair. Rather than being blindsided months or years later, you can address the issue right away. This applies for business as well.

If you notice a change in your relationship with a lead or an existing client, something has changed. Maybe they are making more money, maybe they found a better deal, or they aren't happy with your services. Either way, when you notice a change in the baseline, it's important to follow up and see what caused the change.

> *Personal Experience: There are only so many problems that people can have. When you've worked with people for a long time, you are able to identify their patterns and what they need to fix their solution. If I see someone sad, I know how to get them out of that state. If I see them lacking confidence, I know what I need to do to give them confidence. An example of this was a client of mine told me that he was having trouble with his relationship. His wife was out of rapport with him, they were fighting constantly, and it was affecting his kids.*

After a few moments of him explaining his situation, I was able to identify the problem and give him specific advice on how to address it. A week later when he came back, he was happy, his wife was happy, and his kids were happy. All I had to do was identify the patterns from the data he was telling me.

Triggers and Anchors

When someone changes their baseline, positively or negatively, it's probably not a one-off event. Usually, the cause of someone's change is tied to a trigger or an anchor. You need to start taking note of these triggers. For example, *every time someone is hungry, they act like this. Every time I say this, they act like that.* Simply by noticing this, you can start to direct this person's behavior. If you want to put them in a bad mood, say that one thing. If you want them in a good mood, make sure they eat breakfast before having that difficult conversation.

By understanding a person's triggers, you can gain full control of their emotional state – which is extremely powerful in influencing their actions.

Apply It Now!

Step One: Identify your own patterns. What's your pattern in relationships? What's your pattern when chasing your goals? Everything is a pattern. Good or bad. Up or down. Are your patterns leading to growth or slowing you down? Ask yourself — are my actions hurting or helping my relationships?

Step Two: Identify the patterns of those around you. Are the patterns of your close circle building you up or holding you back? Are you aware of people's patterns and how they affect your ability to influence them?

Step Three: Apply what you know. How can you use someone's pattern to better understand them? If someone is always grumpy when they are hungry, make sure to feed them before asking for a favor. If your customers always buy more in the morning, make sure you and your team are doing most of your sales activity in the morning.

11

KING LOUIS AND THE MESMERIZED PAINTER

Unleashing Your Inner Authority and Confidence Through Hypnosis

In 1745, the Marquise de Pompadour, the official mistress of King Louis XV of France, commissioned Pierre-Francois Oudry, a renowned French artist, to paint a portrait of a young girl named Marie-Louise O'Murphy. The marquise was a patron of the arts and a powerful figure in the French court, and she was eager to have the portrait completed quickly.

However, Oudry was known to be a slow and meticulous painter, and the marquise feared that the project would take too long. To speed up the process, she enlisted the help of a local hypnotist named Charles Mesmer.

Mesmer was known for his ability to induce deep states of relaxation and altered consciousness in his subjects, and the marquise believed that he could use hypnosis to make Oudry more productive. Mesmer agreed to help and began hypnotizing Oudry before each painting session.

Under Mesmer's hypnotic influence, Oudry was able to work for hours without stopping, completing the portrait in just three sittings. The finished work was a masterpiece, capturing the delicate beauty of Marie-Louise O'Murphy and earning Oudry widespread acclaim.

Mesmer was so impressed by Oudry's response to hypnosis that he began experimenting with the technique more extensively. He eventually developed what he called "animal magnetism," which he believed was a natural energy that flowed through all living things and could be harnessed to induce healing and altered states of consciousness.

Mesmer's animal magnetism soon became popular in Parisian society, and he began treating a variety of medical and psychological conditions with his hypnotic techniques. His treatments involved using magnets and other props to direct the flow of animal magnetism and induce hypnotic states in his patients.

Mesmer's methods were controversial and attracted both criticism and fascination from the medical community. Nevertheless, his patients claimed to have experienced significant improvements in their conditions, and he became quite wealthy as a result.

In the end, the commission of a portrait of a young girl led to the creation of a groundbreaking new field of medicine and a wealthy career for Mesmer.

This was the power of hypnosis nearly three centuries ago, and it has only continued to grow. What's interesting is that Mesmer did not teach the painter anything new. He merely unlocked a power that was *already inside of him.*

Creating a New Identity

One of the most powerful things you can do to unlock your inner potential and increase your confidence is to recreate your identity. As we discussed in earlier chapters, your identity and story are the things that shape your beliefs, values, and behaviors. By changing these fundamental elements of who you are, you can change how you see yourself and how others see you.

A key benefit of creating an alternate identity is that it allows us to separate ourselves from our fears and insecurities. When we take on a new persona, we're able to step outside of our own limitations and imagine what we could achieve if we had the courage and confidence to pursue our dreams.

For example, imagine that you're a shy and introverted person who struggles to speak up in social situations. By creating an alternate identity that embodies confidence, charisma, and wit, you're able to take on new roles and identities that would have previously felt impossible. You might find yourself approaching new people with ease, engaging in lively conversations, and taking on leadership roles that you never would have considered before.

But creating an alternate identity isn't just about taking on a new persona — it's also about instilling good behaviors and habits. When we create a persona that embodies the qualities we want to cultivate in ourselves, we're more likely to embody those qualities in our everyday lives.

If you create an alternate identity that embodies discipline and focus, you may find it easier to stick to a strict workout routine or complete a challenging work project.

At its core, creating an alternate identity is a powerful tool for personal growth and development. By tapping into our imaginations and envisioning new versions of ourselves, we can push past our limitations and discover new sources of creativity, inspiration, and success.

How To Create Your Alternate Identity:

1. **Identify the qualities you want to embody:** Start by thinking about the qualities you want to embody as a confident and authoritative person. Do you want to

be more assertive? Calmer and more composed? More charismatic and inspiring? Write down the qualities you want to embody.

2. **Create a script:** Once you have identified the qualities you want to embody, create a hypnosis script that focuses on these qualities. Your script should be positive, affirming, and focused on the present moment. For example, "I am confident and assertive in all situations" or "I am calm and composed, even in stressful situations."

Start Walking in Your New Identity

Once you've created an alternate identity, you have to start walking in that new persona. Once you start practicing being the "new you," you will start building unbreakable confidence in your life. Simply imagining your alternate identity is not enough — you must also take action to bring that persona to life.

One of the best ways to do this is through the practice of "walking in your new shoes." This means adopting the physical posture, mannerisms, and behaviors of your alternate identity in your everyday life. By walking, speaking, and interacting like your alternate identity, you're able to embody their confidence, authority, and charisma.

For example, if your alternate identity is a confident and charismatic speaker, practice giving speeches or presentations in their style. If your alternate identity is a disciplined and focused athlete, practice your workouts and training sessions in their mindset. The more you practice embodying your alternate identity, the more natural and effortless it will become.

Walking in your new shoes also helps to create a sense of separation between yourself and your alternate identity. This separation can be beneficial for two reasons: first, it allows you to step outside of your own limitations and fears and imagine what you could achieve if you had the confidence and authority of your alternate identity.

Second, it allows you to maintain a healthy sense of self-awareness and self-reflection, ensuring that your alternate identity remains a positive force for change in your life.

Ultimately, the importance of walking in your new alternate identity lies in the power of embodied cognition. Our physical actions and behaviors have a profound effect on our thoughts, emotions, and beliefs. By adopting the physical posture and behaviors of our alternate identity, we're able to shift our mindset and embody the traits and characteristics we want to cultivate in ourselves.

If you want to be confident and successful in your new alternate identity, don't just imagine it — walk in your new shoes and bring that persona to life.

Maintaining Your Alternate Personality

The easiest way to solidify your new identity is to start walking in it.

Caring for your alternate personality is equally as important as creating the new identity. This is a simple but crucial process. Taking the time to put yourself in an environment where you are constantly challenged to improve, to walk in confidence, and be that person you need to be will help you to maintain your new personality.

Keep feeding your new identity with activities, goals, and new connections that help you grow into the new role. This might involve delving into meditation, pursuing therapy, or joining support groups that champion self-care and personal growth.

By embracing and nurturing your alternate personality with the care it deserves, you'll unlock an extraordinary inner world that bleeds into your outer world in the form of confidence and success.

Unbreakable Peak State

Creating a new identity, hypnotizing yourself, and walking in your new identity can be a powerful way to tap into your full potential and achieve a state of unstoppable confidence and authority. This journey is not just about taking on a new persona; it's about transforming yourself into the best version of yourself.

The ultimate goal of this process is to achieve a peak state — a state of mind where you feel invincible, powerful, and unstoppable. In this state, anything is possible, and you're capable of achieving your wildest dreams. Your alternate identity represents your highest self, and stepping into that persona can unlock new levels of creativity, inspiration, and success.

The road to a peak state can be challenging, but it's also incredibly rewarding. By creating an alternate identity, you're giving yourself permission to step outside of your comfort zone and explore new parts of your personality.

By hypnotizing yourself, you're unlocking the power of your subconscious mind and tapping into hidden reserves of creativity and inspiration. And by walking in your new identity, you're embodying the confidence, authority, and charisma that you've always wanted.

When you achieve a peak state, you'll gain massive confidence and authority in your personal and professional life. People will look up to you as a leader and an authority figure, and you'll be seen as a force to be reckoned with. You'll be able to take on new challenges with ease, inspire others to follow your lead, and achieve your wildest dreams.

Remember that creating an alternate identity is a journey of self-discovery and personal transformation. It's a chance to explore new parts of yourself, take on new roles and identities, and tap into hidden reserves of creativity and inspiration. By following these steps and committing to the process, you can achieve a peak state and become the best version of yourself.

Raise Your Standards

When you raise your standards, life changes instantly. It doesn't change tomorrow, it doesn't change in a year, it changes the moment that you decide you will do whatever you must do to raise your standards. The problem is that most people don't realize how easy it is to raise your standards. Raising your standards is not wanting to make more money, live a better life, or be healthier.

Raising your standards is a need. When you raise your standards, you are telling yourself that *I need (fill in the blank) to survive.* When you say this about happiness, peace, health, finances, your brain immediately will look for ways to survive.

Some of us have convinced ourselves that it's easier to stay put than to raise our standards. It's not. Working out at the gym is a lot easier than having a heart attack because you were unhealthy. It's easier to make more money than it is to make less money. Going through chemotherapy and radiation therapy is a lot harder than just eating a little bit healthier.

Raise your standards, take control of your life, and be who you always wanted to be.

Walking In Real Confidence

You build confidence by doing things that are uncomfortable. Doing this habitually will naturally build confidence. This works because your brain is scared of novelty. The more you train your brain that it doesn't have to be scared of novelty, the more confident you will feel and appear.

The problem that occurs is that we usually are attracted to, and attempt to act with, confidence that isn't real. It's fake. Think of the phrase "liquid courage." People often use drugs or alcohol to induce a state of confidence, but this actually shows that they are the opposite. Essentially, their brains are telling them *I can't be myself unless I drink. When I drink then I am confident to be myself.* Drugs and alcohol don't make you confident; they just block the feelings of shyness, fear, etc.

In fact, you will often find that the opposite is true. If someone doesn't drink or do drugs, they are probably more confident. Why? Because they don't need to disassociate themselves from the feeling of being a coward in order to have a fun time and be themselves.

The point of all of this is simple: Don't run away from discomfort. Run to it and train your brain to be comfortable in uncomfortable situations.

Apply It Now:

1. **Create Your Alternate Identity:** Who do you want to be? How does this person talk, dress and act? Is this person kind or disagreeable? Is this person gentle-spoken or a bit of a loudmouth? Be very specific.

2. **Determine what actions you need to take to become this person:** Right now, you need to choose an action that will help solidify this alter-identity in your mind.. Right down the action and go do it as soon as possible. If you don't, you are further engraining the old, version of yourself that is incapable of taking you to the next step in your life.

3. **Find An Accountability Partner:** This is an important step. Find someone you can trust who will hold you accountable to your new identity. Anytime they see you acting out of character, they need to remind you of who you are. Make sure this person is honest but also knows how to keep you motivated.

12

FINAL THOUGHTS
Putting the Pieces Together

Most of us think that it takes years of some crazy morning routine to build the life of our dreams. I simply don't believe that. Whether you are just starting out as an entrepreneur or have a monthly income of millions of dollars, more confidence will allow you to take your life to the next level in business, relationships, and personal growth. Gaining unstoppable confidence is the key to taking control of your life.

I've had the opportunity to see firsthand how gaining crazy confidence can change someone's life in an instant. From witnessing one of my good friends being healed of a deadly case of cancer, to seeing a client quit smoking in 30 seconds, to seeing CEOs and entrepreneurs take their companies from nothing to seven and eight figures — the power of hypnosis is real, and you can access it too.

It's my biggest goal to see the techniques that I have used and taught others transform as many lives as I possibly can. I don't have some arbitrary number in mind like wanting to change a million lives or whatever in my lifetime... But I do want to change the world. There is so much more I could teach, but I wanted to write a book that you could read through and apply the information instantly.

I'll probably end up writing book two to help those of you who read this book take your abilities to the next level. But I do want to make sure I leave you with this. Since you've completed this book, you are now ready to do the following:

1. You are ready to take control of your own thoughts and emotions and take the driver's seat in your mind. By doing this, you will start to walk with more purpose, clarity, and most importantly, confidence.

2. I've shared some of the tips that have allowed me to build a multi-million-dollar business and I've done it for the low cost of this book. You are more than ready to apply this in your own life and build your own empire.

3. Lastly, I need you to know that I am always here for you. If you need more help in your life or your business relationships, you can always reach me for more. I've committed my whole life to helping people just like you.

If you want more...

If you want more motivation in life, you can find me on **Instagram**. I'm constantly dropping tips for how to find happiness and love — plus it will give first access to a lot of my private masterminds and other events. You can find me there by searching **@marczell.**

If you're looking for tactics and strategies, my **YouTube** channel goes into more detail on many of the topics I share on Instagram. I normally upload several videos a week here. Just search for my channel "Marczell Klein."

If you are looking for direct access to me, my **website** is the best place to go. With information about my courses, live events, and 1-1 coaching, this is the perfect place if you are looking to get to the next level even faster.

Sources:

Introduction

Milgram, S. *Behavioral study of obedience.* Journal of Abnormal and Social Psychology, 67, 371-378. (1963).

Milgram, S. *Some conditions of obedience and disobedience to authority.* Human Relations, *18(1)*, 57-76. (1965).

Chapter One

Roth, Adam. *The Man Who Cured Cancer With His Mind.* Journal of Projective Techniques, Vol. 21, Issue 4. (1957).

Chapter Two

Smith, Brendan. *Hypnosis Today.* American Psychological Association, Vol. 42, No. 1. (January 2011).

Chapter Four

O'Flynn, Kevin. *Russian bank robber hypnotized tellers.* MinnPost. Dec. 15, 2009.

Chapter Five

Jones, Earnest. The Life and Work of Sigmund Freud. Jan. 9, 1953.

Chapter Seven

Marty Homlish Takes SAP's Message to the World. CMO.co m, 20 November 2012.

SAP CMO Marty Homlish on Digital Marketing and the Customer Experience. Econsultancy, 12 February 2013.

The CMO Files: Marty Homlish, SAP. ZDNet, 28 May 2018.

Chapter Eight

The Last and Greatest Battle: Finding the Will, Commitment, and Strategy to End Military Suicides. John Bateson Oxford University Press, 2015.

Killing does not come easy for soldiers. The Washington Post. Oct. 13, 2017.

SLA Marshall - Men Against Fire: The Problem of Battle Command

Chapter Nine

Finnegan, William. *When the Unabomber Was Arrested, One of the Longest Manhunts in FBI History Was Finally Over.* Smithsonian Magazine. May 2018.

Chapter Ten

Braid, James. *The Discovery of Hypnosis: The Complete Writings of James Braid, the Father of Hypnotherapy.* Lulu. August 2013.

www.ingramcontent.com/pod-product-compliance
Lightning Source LLC
Chambersburg PA
CBHW060240030426
42335CB00014B/1549